What Your Handwriting Tells About You

What Your Handwriting Tells About You

Joan Hake Robie

Broadman Press
Nashville, Tennessee

Dedication

To My Family

Charles

David

Daniel

4269-22
ISBN: 0-8054-6922-2

Dewey Decimal Classification: 137
Subject heading: GRAPHOANALYSIS
Library of Congress Catalog Card Number: 77-91726
Printed in the United States of America

Contents

1. It Is Written   7
2. First Things First   13
3. Dale Evans Rogers   17
4. Pat Boone   24
5. T's Tell Tall Tales   29
6. Jane Withers   36
7. Robert H. Schuller   41
8. Troubled Kids   46
9. The Humbards   60
10. Look Up, Look Down   67
11. Betsy Palmer   72
12. Norma Zimmer   77
13. Your Emotions Are Showing   80
14. What's Your Beat?   95
15. Can You Spot a Criminal?   98
16. Colonel Harland Sanders   104
17. Kathryn Kuhlman   111
18. Their Writing Talks   115
        Cliff Barrows   116
        Dave Boyer   117
        Bill Brown   118
        Joan Winmill Brown   119
        President Jimmy Carter   120
        Judson Cornwall   121

Andraé Crouch   122
Richard M. DeVos   123
David DuPlessis   124
Joni Eareckson   125
Billy Graham   126
Ruth Graham   127
Hansi   128
Al Hartley   129
The Hawaiians   130
Charles Hunter   131
Frances Hunter   132
Elisabeth Elliot Leitch   133
Pat Robertson   134
George Beverly Shea   135
Jimmy Swaggart   136
Ethel Waters   137
David Wilkerson   138

19. True Confessions   139

1.
It Is Written

Dale Evans Rogers was deserted by her husband. Colonel Harland D. Sanders of Kentucky Fried Chicken fame was a 6th-grade school dropout. Norma Zimmer's mother was an alcoholic. But each of these well-known personalities has made an unusual and significant contribution to our society.

We all hope for success in life. To one person success is an abundance of money. To another, success is good health. To still another, success is to be loved. The famous movie actress, Miss Bette Davis, has said, "If within yourself you have lived up to an ideal you have for your life and have won your goal—that is success." But wishing for success and attaining it are on opposite sides of a pole. Some people never reach their goals. Why? Some "cop out" by blaming someone else.

In spite of her "hard luck," Dale Evans Rogers became an internationally known actress and singer. Colonel Sanders made millions of dollars after the age when most people retire by promoting his "secret" recipe for fried chicken. Norma Zimmer became an outstanding singer on the *Lawrence Welk Show* on television.

Each of us come into this world with our own unique talents. It is up to us, with God's help, to make the best of what we have—no matter the odds. Some of your qualities or traits might be strong and positive influences on your life, while other less desirable ones might keep you at the brink of success for the rest of your life. You never cross over to reach that goal. In Luke 19 of the Holy Scriptures we read about the nobleman who gave his assistants money to invest. Two of the men invested the money and came back with the profits. The third man did nothing with the money. He just kept it. Then, that which he had was taken away from him. The nobleman was angered by the assistant's lack of wisdom and foresight.

What was it that made one man do nothing with what he had when the other two men made good use of their talents? We can agree that he had no vision.

Certain negative personality traits, if not overpowered by positive ones, can be the cause of conflict and struggle. As we look at people like Dale Evans Rogers, Colonel Sanders, and Norma Zimmer, we ask, "What made them reach their goals? How did they do it?"

One approach to learning the makeup of a person is to take a look at, or to study, his personality. There are various avenues for doing this. One way is to examine his handwriting. A handwriting specialist or analyst is often asked, "Can you really tell what a person is like from reading his signature? If I give you something I have written, can you tell my future? Whom will I marry? Will I become rich?"

People are interested in knowing about themselves. They are interested in knowing about those they love. Husbands want to know about their wives. Wives want to know about their husbands. Parents want to know about their children.

Because of the confusion which exists regarding the effectiveness of handwriting analysis, some people are inclined to think that handwriting analysis is some sort of magic or involved with the occult. But this assumption is incorrect. A true handwriting analyst does not make predictions about the future. Handwriting analysis is a science used to determine personality traits, to declare a document valid or invalid, to help a physician in the diagnosis of an illness, and for many other purposes. The science of handwriting analysis is a subdivision of psychology, with acceptance and accredited courses offered in universities around the world. There are estimated to be over twenty thousand psychologists, psychiatrists, teachers, clergymen, and other professional associates who are using handwriting every day to gain a better insight into clients and then to help these clients make a better adjustment in life.

Handwriting is "brain-writing." It is a neuromuscular activity through which the brain projects visual thought symbols on a sheet of paper. It can be likened to the electrocardiograph which measures the pattern of the heartbeat. In other words, it is a physical act which requires the full use of the mind. A person's state of mind is reflected in the way he writes. When your spirits are low and your feet drag, likewise your pen sags. Your personality, your emotions, your intellect, your energy are at the stub of your pen.

We are all individuals with unique personalities and, thus, our writing is never exactly the same. This is why no two persons write in exactly the same manner. People tell me that their handwriting changes from day to day and therefore it can't be analyzed correctly. This is not true, because the basic characteristics of a handwriting remain the same. What changes is the writer's moods, and the script will vary in its slant and scope. A professional graphoanalyst could recognize this as the same handwriting, no matter on what day, or in what mood, it was written. It would not matter whether the writing instrument were held in the hand, between the teeth, or between the toes of the foot. Beautifully etched scenes are done for greeting cards by a young woman who has no use of her arms or hands. The scenes are created as she works with a pen held between her teeth. We will find out more about her later on in the book.

Ever since mid-Renaissance, when Camillo Baldi, an Italian physician, wrote the first treatise on the subject, many learned persons became convinced that handwriting can indicate character traits. Another observation was made by the Roman author, Tranquilius. He noted that Emperor Caesar Augustus was so economical that he squeezed his words together at the end of one line rather than start a new line. Sigmund Freud wrote, "There is no doubt that men also express their character through their handwriting." It is only within the last century, however, that serious attention has been paid to this social science.

Even though many of us learned to write by the Palmer method, there are no two identical handwritings. Although children are taught by the same penmanship book there are "good writers" and "poor writers." A perfect handwriting does not mean a perfect personality. The writer might be too conforming and conventional.

Later in this book we will get to know some of the personality traits which make up the celebrity, Dale Evans Rogers, singer, actress, and wife of cowboy Roy Rogers. If anyone knows what hard times can be, it's Dale. Married in her early teens, Dale was on her way to a life of hardship and misery. While her son was still an infant, Dale's husband left her and she became disillusioned and bitter. In spite of all her problems, Dale made sure her son went to Sunday School where he would receive religious training. Life would bring another marriage and another failure, but Dale had the qualities to keep her going through it all.

Jane Withers' mother had a dream that her daughter would some day be a star. Nothing would stop Mrs. Withers from making that dream become a reality. So she packed suitcases, took her daughter, and headed for the show-biz capital of the world. Little wonder that her daughter, Jane, would grow to be a woman of strength and purpose.

The late Ethel Waters' life was full of frustration and heart-ache. She was miserably overweight. The years had crept upon her when she met the Savior, but her life took on meaning. She lost the excess weight, gained her health and strength, and met a person who would become a good friend, Billy Graham.

Pat Boone wanted to finish an education, but it wasn't easy to work his way through college and support a wife and four baby girls. Pat's determination made it possible for him to graduate from college and begin an exciting career as a singer and actor.

Few of us would be willing to make the kind of sacrifices Colonel Harland Sanders did. The Colonel is the founder of Kentucky Fried Chicken. Would we be willing to do like Colonel Sanders did at age sixty-five, start out on a new profession, at night sleeping in the backseat of our automobile, and getting up in the morning stiff and aching in our bones to face restaurant owners who would slam doors in our faces? As you read the Colonel Sanders story you will recognize some of the personality traits which helped make him a successful man.

Lawrence Welk's "Champagne Lady," singer Norma Zimmer, was the pride and joy of her father. When Norma's musical talent began to surface, her father saw to it that she was headed for a career in that field. No outside influence would deter his daughter from reaching that goal.

Rex Humbard had a rich heritage, not materially but spiritually. His mother and father spent their time traveling the continent singing and preaching the gospel. Their children were taught to play musical instruments and when they were ready they began performing on the church circuit.

Mystery surrounded the earlier life of the late Evangelist Kathryn Kuhlman. There is said to have been a marriage which failed but until her recent book was written little else was known. Feeling the call of God, Miss Kuhlman gave the greater part of her life in service to others. This is why she will never be forgotten by those who had the privilege of knowing her and her ministry.

Dr. Robert Schuller is a man who believes in possibility thinking, so much so that even in the face of odds he keeps his chin up—like the time he had an accident and had to be taken by ambulance to a hospital. His positive faith kept him happy and hopeful as he pondered how this experience could benefit him and others.

Throughout this book we will look closer at many of these celebrities. Many will share their own experiences. We will analyze their handwriting and find out what personality traits they reveal.

We will also study a fascinating art—the analysis of handwriting (or graphoanalysis). Yes, WHAT YOUR HANDWRITING TELLS ABOUT YOU is captivating and intriguing.

2.
First Things First

There are possibly four hundred factors of personality in various degrees of strength and frequency which reveal certain traits to a professional graphoanalyst. The handwriting expert is able to determine the emotional makeup of a person's will-power, intelligence, potential, expression, and his adjustment to life. The analyst does this by observing things like slant, pressure, letter size, margins, zones, rhythm, spacing, signature, I-dots, and T-bars.

The size of the writing is one of the first things to consider when analyzing it. Size is a gauge to the writer's intellect, ability to concentrate, and aptness for details. Large writing which is composed of expansive, flamboyant letters usually reveals a person who enjoys activity and achievement, seeing and being seen. This type of person is always on the go. He doesn't like to be bogged down with details. It takes self-assurance to write large. There is a tendency or desire to be lavish. However, abnormally large writing usually signifies ostentation, arrogance, and a desire to dominate others.

Most people write in medium size. Because it is nothing unusual, its significance will not be clear until we consider it in relation to other factors in the writing, things like legibility, slant, and other characteristics.

A handwriting which is small indicates a person who sees the world close at hand. He is thorough, concise, and interested in details. The small writing requires patience and concentration. People who write small might like to remain somewhat aloof from others. A scientist, student, or philosopher might write small. Unusually small writing denotes stinginess on the part of the writer.

The handwriting of people who are versatile will be likely to vary in size, according to their moods. When they are happy, they might form extra large letters; when they are concentrating on a problem their writing might be much smaller. However, even if the size of the writing varies, other factors in the writing will reveal basic personality traits.

Optimism and pessimism are revealed in the base line of a handwriting. The best way to analyze a writing is when the writing is done on unlined paper. When you examine the writing just imagine there is a base line drawn across the sheet of paper, and determine whether the writing proceeds on an even line or whether it pulls from this imaginary line.

Handwriting which consistently goes across the sheet in a straight line belongs to a person who is not easily swayed by outside influences, such as the opinions of others. He maintains his "cool."

Optimism is expressed when the line of handwriting ascends. This writer is not easily discouraged. He maintains a hopeful outlook on life and is generally an ambitious individual. People who write uphill adapt themselves socially. If the writing goes uphill at a very extreme angle, the individual is the kind of person who keeps his head so far up in the clouds that he doesn't always use good judgment. Nevertheless, he is usually a happy person, that is, if other traits reinforce this one.

Pessimism is evident when a handwriting descends consistently. This person does not display enthusiasm or hopefulness over new ideas, and he is likely to become skeptical when they are expressed. If the downhill slant is not too marked, the pessimism may be a mixture of caution and critical faculty. It is not an unhappy trait. A downhill slant at a very sharp angle is a sign of a confirmed pessimist. It is difficult to get him out of his groove of depression.

We must note, though, that pessimism can sometimes be only a temporary state, and it is best to examine previous samples of the writing to see whether the downward lines are done consistently, or whether the earlier specimens show a straight or uphill base line. The most cheerful person has times when he may go through an experience which causes depression and instinctively causes the writing to descend. When he has passed through the difficult time, it is amazing how the line of writing will spring back up to its normal straight or uphill slant.

A person of variable moods may change the base line of his writing with each word or with each line or with each page of writing. This person's moods change constantly, according to the time, place, and companions. This type of person might find it difficult to become adjusted to any work or hobby which calls for routine.

The experienced handwriting analyst is able to determine the emotional makeup of a person's willpower, intelligence, potential, expression, and his adjustment to life. The analyst does this by observing, not only the size of the writing and the ascension or descension of the line of writing, but other things like margins, rhythm, spacing, pressure, and more.

Handwriting analysis can be a great help in our understanding of each other. It offers an individual a means of objective self-evaluation for self-improvement purposes—of course, not to the exclusion of the power of God and prayer. Handwriting analysis is a valuable tool in occupations such as family counseling, teaching, personnel selection, and other activities where being able to predict an individual's behavior, as a result of understanding his personality, is usually beneficial. Police use this tool in helping to identify a criminal. Later in this book we give some examples of how handwriting analysis helps to find a forger. Also, the examination of questioned documents such as the signatures on wills is another service offered by the trained analyst. The handwriting analyst has a great responsibility to his client and to himself.

You might not be a professional handwriting analyst, but by the time you have finished reading this book you should be able to look at someone's writing and have a better understanding of what is revealed. *When you look at each celebrity's writing, see if you can analyze it before you look at the given analysis.*

3.
Dale Evans Rogers

"From the time I was a little girl I wanted to sing and be in show business," says Western star Dale Evans Rogers. "I sang my first public solo in the Baptist church when I was nine years old. I sang my mother's favorite hymn, 'In the Garden.' "

When Dale was ten years old, an evangelist came to her church. At the close of one service, after the evangelist had explained that there was a heaven and a hell and Jesus was the key to heaven, Dale raised her hand, indicating that she wanted to be "saved."

"I believed that Jesus was able to save me," says Dale, "but I didn't give him my life. I was like a person who was taking out an insurance policy which would guarantee her heaven when she died. Now I see that that was the worst mistake I ever made in my entire life—by not giving him the reins of my life. As a result, I became rebellious against my parents and eloped with my first sweetheart when I was in my early teens. That just about broke my parents' hearts.

"We had a child, and while our little boy Tom was still an infant, my husband deserted me. He said he wanted to be free and that our marriage had been a mistake and that we were both very young."

Dale Evans, born Frances Octavia Smith, was deeply hurt, and became bitter and disillusioned. Forced to get a divorce that she did not want, she decided that no one would ever have the opportunity to hurt her again. She would aim for worldly success and financial security for herself and her young son.

Later, after taking a business course she moved to Memphis, Tennessee, where she took a job as a secretary. But her real ambition was to sing on the radio. Her insurance-agent boss used to hear her singing while she typed claim forms. Since he had a program on a small radio station, he "dared" Dale to go down to the station one night and sing on radio. This resulted in Dale's getting a weekly Friday night program. Doors began to open and soon she was singing for civic groups and wherever else she was asked.

"All the while I took my little boy to Sunday School because I wanted him to have the spiritual security that I wasn't willing to take for myself. I was afraid to give my life to God because I thought I would get hurt again and wouldn't be able to make a name for myself and thus establish that security I felt I needed for my son and me."

Dale Evans decided to go to Chicago but the time was during the Great Depression, and she couldn't get a job singing on radio. She took what work she was able to find, but things didn't go well and as a result her health broke and she was forced to go back to her home in Texas. Later she landed a radio job in Louisville, Kentucky, where she performed on a program called "The Early Bird Program." Later, she joined a dance band.

Dale recalls, "During the time I was living and working on radio in Louisville, Kentucky, there was an epidemic of infantile paralysis. One day I came home from the studio and found my son with a violent headache and vomiting. The muscles of his legs were drawing up, and he was screaming with aches in his limbs. He'd been taken to the doctor who was pretty sure my son had infantile paralysis. Tom was put into the hospital where a spinal tap was performed to determine whether or not he had the disease. There I stood, watching them put a long needle in my son who didn't even whimper. He was a godly boy and lived such a life of consecration before me. I know now that the Lord gave me this boy to keep me in line—from wandering too far. I loved this boy so much. He was gifted in music and loved the Lord, the church, and Sunday School.

"Realizing the desperate situation which faced my boy I prayed, 'Lord, please don't let my boy have infantile paralysis. If you will spare him and let the tests be negative, I'll follow you and put you first in my life.' I was so relieved when my prayers were answered and the tests were negative. But all too soon I forgot my promise to God, and again ambition got the best of me."

Says Dale, "I tried marriage again, but again it was a failure. The reason was that I had never learned to love or trust anyone. I didn't know how to love because 'God is love,' and when we have him in our hearts we learn how to love. Then we can take opposition from other people and understand that Christ died for them. 'Having done all, we can stand' in our marriage and stay with it. But at that time I didn't understand the meaning of those words."

Dale went back to Chicago where she got a job singing at the Balinese Room and the Drake Hotel, the Ché Paree, and finally CBS. One night a Hollywood agent heard her sing and later gave her a screen test. She landed a job with Twentieth Century-Fox which gave her a year's contract. During World War II she worked hard entertaining the troops.

"Then my agent told me I couldn't let people know I had a son because that would make me appear too old. He said I'd have to send my boy away to school. But I told him 'No way will I do that.' Then, my agent announced, 'He's your brother!' Neither my son nor I liked this kind of deception, but that was what my agent decided."

For Dale Evans the next years brought her increased success. "The Chase and Sanborn Hour" which she did for forty-three weeks, then a musical with Lula Bell and Scottie from the

"Barn Dance" in Chicago, and then she was chosen leading lady for a rising young star named Roy Rogers. This was to be followed by a long list of pictures with Roy Rogers.

"When I went to Hollywood I made up my mind that I would make lots of money and that no one would ever hurt me or my boy again. I would make enough money to give him a fine musical education and to live a comfortable life. Most of all I wanted him to be safe and secure in Jesus Christ. I wanted my son to have what I wouldn't take for myself. I'd go to Sunday School and church with him, and the preacher would talk about people who had gifts that God had given them but wouldn't let the Lord use those gifts. I'd get angry inside and be convicted, but I wouldn't let the Lord have my life. It was because I was afraid I'd have to give up my career. I really was afraid I'd be called to be a missionary."

Dale's life took a whole new turn when, on New Year's Eve, 1947, she became the wife of her leading man, Roy Rogers, a widower with three children—a little girl seven years old, a girl five years old, and a baby boy who was only fifteen months old.

"As I was dressing to be married, the Spirit of the Lord God fell upon me, and I was convicted in my heart of my sins of omission as well as commission—for failing God by not following him—heartaches I had caused myself and others by not yielding my life to Jesus Christ.

"I remember how, before my marriage to Roy, I went into a closet and shut the door. There I prayed, 'Lord, please give me the courage to establish a Christian home for Roy and his children. Help me in this marriage or I'll never make it. You know that I don't have the ability, in myself, to make it.'

"Then I went in to be married. After that we went back to Hollywood to establish a home. My son, Tom, lived with us, along with Roy's three children. Within two or three months things were not going so well. After our marriage I had been taken out of Roy's pictures. I'd been a career woman since I was seventeen years old and I found it difficult to adjust to my new way of life. Roy's children resented me as a stepmother coming into the home and taking over. I was having a lot of problems because I didn't really have the Lord in my life.

"One day my son came into my room and caught me crying. He said, 'Come to church with me tonight. You owe it to Roy's children to establish a Christian home.' I did go to church that night, and it was the greatest decision I ever made. That night the preacher preached a sermon that I shall never forget. It was about the home that is built on the rock of faith in Jesus Christ. The preacher said that that kind of home would never fail, no matter what kind of storm lashed against it, because it was built on sure, solid rock. When the sermon was over, my son turned to me and said, 'Mom, give your life to Christ.' I answered, 'I am a Christian. I accepted him when I was ten.' My son continued, 'But you don't *know* him. Just accepting him as Savior and not having a vital personal relationship with him day by day is not the same thing.'

"In my search for release from my nervous tension I had read all kinds of books—books on Eastern philosophies and many other subjects in order to ease my guilt complex—but nothing helped. I was miserable inside, fearful inside, sick to my soul.

"Nevertheless, I turned to my son and said, 'Let me think about it.'

"I went home that night and knelt by my bed. Then, the Lord unrolled my life just like a carpet in front of me. It wasn't a pretty sight. I cried out to God and said, 'O Lord, have mercy on me. If you let me live until next Sunday, I will publicly acknowledge you, and you can have the rest of my life and use me as you see fit.'

"The next Sunday I literally ran down the aisle when they gave the invitation. Then I shook the minister's hand and went into a prayer room with a lady I didn't know. There we knelt and I poured out my heart to the Lord and said, 'Lord, come into my life, forgive my sin by the blood you shed on the cross of Calvary. Wash me clean, Lord, and break my life if you have to, but use the rest of my life.'

"I walked out of that church a new person. I felt so wonderful that I can't express just how I felt. It was as though I were ten feet tall and walking on air. The trees were greener, the flowers were more beautiful, and I felt love in my heart for everyone; even people I didn't like. For the first time in my life I was really happy. I had found peace at last."

DALE EVANS ROGERS

Dale Evans Rogers' intensely emotional nature is not always the same in its response to experiences. Dale is a woman who is usually in a hurry, and she has lots of physical drive and persistence. Her flair for the sensational and flamboyant makes her comfortable in front of an audience. Her generous nature explains her concern for others. This multitalented woman enjoys people and thrives on love and attention. She is very imaginative and has a mysterious and cautious side to her nature. In spite of this, she is likely to say what she thinks.

4.

Pat Boone

"For years I thought of myself as a Christian," says singer/actor Pat Boone, "because I had named the name of the Lord when I was thirteen years old. I had been baptized and thought of myself as a pretty good guy."

Pat, a direct descendent of frontiersman Daniel Boone, was born in 1934, one of four children. After emceeing for a high school talent show on radio, he won top honors for his performances on the "Ted Mack Amateur Hour" and the "Arthur Godfrey Talent Scout" show.

Later, Pat worked as a disc jockey which led to a contract with Dot Records, and on to a series of successful records and a job with Arthur Godfrey.

Married to the daughter of the late and great Red Foley, Pat became the father of four daughters. All the while he studied at Columbia University, graduating magna cum laude. In 1956 he signed a million-dollar contract with Twentieth Century-Fox for one picture a year for seven years. Pat's records have sold more than thirty million copies.

Pat continues, "Most people agreed with me that I was a pretty good guy." (Pat has been known through the years for his white buckskin shoes.) "But behind the scenes I had really gotten away from God, and I'd gotten to the point where I thought that if I had some money in the bank, nice clothes to wear, and could make a record now and then I'd be OK. I thought I'd help God out in my spare time.

"However, a few years ago I found that if God wasn't breathing into my life I couldn't handle my career, the money, or anything else. The more I tried to hold onto my possessions, the more they seemed to slip away.

"My career was 'cooling off.' Not only that, but I'd gotten involved in so many business problems that with one giant problem I was about to go bankrupt. Here was Pat Boone, ready to lose everything. This brought me to my knees, because, all of a sudden, after fifteen years as an entertainer, I thought I was going to lose it all.

"I had thought that I was so important to God and could do so many great things for him. Now, I was going to be stripped of everything. I had nothing left to give him, except my heart and soul, and to give myself in a way that I'd never done before. I began to seek God and pray, getting away by myself. 'Lord,' I prayed one day, 'It looks like just about everything I thought I had to give you is being taken away. All I've got now is to give you myself. I hope you'll just take me and use me, 'cause otherwise I really have nothing. All of my successes have been in vain.'

"One day I went up on a hilltop in Beverly Hills, California, with a dear friend, Reverend Harald Bredesen. There on that hilltop I had an experience with God like I'd never had before. Harald and I went up there to pray. It was great! If we wanted to cry, we could cry; if we wanted to shout, we could shout. There was nobody around to hear or see or interrupt us. We didn't have to worry about being embarrassed. It was just us and God.

"That experience had a profound effect on my life and when we had finished praying Harald asked me a very nitty, gritty question. He said, 'Pat, are you willing to die to your career if that is what God wants of you?' That was the last thing in the world that I wanted to hear. That was the last question I ever wanted anybody to ask me, 'Will you die to your career if that is what God wants?'

"Well, I thought it over. I thought, 'Man, I don't think I

have too much career left to die to.' At least it looked that way at the time. What little I had I wanted to hang onto, but I knew that if I hung onto my career and didn't have God I'd still have nothing. So I said, 'Harald, if I know my own heart and soul I am willing to die to my career. Whatever God wants me to do I'll do. If he wants me to pump gas in Pomona, teach school in Tennessee, hold a street meeting in Harlem, or whatever else he wants me to do, I'm willing to do it because I know that I'll be happy. So if it means giving up my career I'll do it.'

"Then Harald said, 'God is not going to let you stay down in the dumps where you are now. He's going to solve your problems. He's going to lift you up, because in the fourth chapter of James we read that when we really seek God and draw near to him, he will draw near to us.

"Later, when I was back home, my business adviser came to me and said, 'Pat, it's all over. The bank is going to take everything you've got. You'd better be prepared for a lot of jokes in the entertainment business. We give up. We can't do any more. It looks like it's all over.'

"Then, Shirley and I looked at him and said, 'God's got this problem in his hands. Don't worry.'

"He answered, 'But the bank's got it in its hands.' And we answered, 'God's got the bank in his hands.'

"I want to praise God for what happened later because it was a two-million-dollar miracle. A man from Washington, D.C., came to us with two million dollars in his hand. My partner and I hadn't even known that this man existed. For his own reasons, he came to buy the Oakland basketball team which we owned and as a result lifted the heavy burden right off our shoulders. It was a miracle, just as much as the parting of the Red Sea. But the greatest miracle was the one that happened in my life and the life of my family."

After twenty years, Pat Boone is still hitting the top headlines. He played the part of David Wilkerson in the movie version of *The Cross and the Switchblade*. Suddenly, it seemed that all his old movies were being shown on TV, and the Pat Boone Family Singers—Shirley, Cherry, Lindy, Debby, Laury, and Pat—have become one of the most popular groups of the day. God has a way of turning problems into promises that turn into glorious reality.

Hi Joan!

...ind the dead in Christ shall rise first —

...en we which are alive and remain shall be caught up together with them in the air — and so shall we ever be with the Lord.

Pat Boone

PAT BOONE

Pat Boone enjoys being in the limelight. His determination and persistence, added to his sense of independence, make him an achiever. He is likely to reach his goals in life. He is a man who is keenly aware and possesses intuitive powers. His moves are usually made with extreme caution. He will investigate a situation and dig out those facts which interest him. The rest he will skim over. At times he is unpredictable in his emotional responses, but generally he will express how he feels about something. A broad-minded individualist, he will give the other fellow the benefit of the doubt. At times his generosity could cause him to be extravagant.

5.
T's Tell Tall Tales

The small letter *t* tells more about a writer than any other single letter. With the small *t* you have a stem. A t-stem can be tall or short; it may be crossed with a bar that is written above the t-stem, or just above the small letters in the writing, or it may be halfway up the stem. The bar which crosses the *t* may be heavy, light, long, or short, or the crossbar may not even be a bar, but a stroke which ties.

All of these variations provide an opportunity for you to determine the truth about a writer's vanity, sensitivity, tenacity, enthusiasm, and many other important character traits.

VANITY: *Exaggerated t-stem height*

You know this person when he brags about his past accomplishments and future plans. He really has no intention of ever following through with these plans, but he likes to hear himself talk. "Every man at his best state is altogether vanity" (Ps. 39:5, Pilgrim Edition).

SELF-BLAME: *T-bars are made from right to left*

He is reserved and withdrawn. Thoughts are directed inward. He is apt to blame himself for things that go wrong. He makes a habit of beating himself down.

"If I justify myself, mine own mouth shall condemn me: if I say, I am perfect, it shall also prove me perverse" (Job 9:20).

SENSITIVENESS: *Looped t-stem*

To be sensitive is neither good nor bad, but it is a liability.

The sensitive person thrives on praise and is always overly alert for the approval or disapproval of others. He is unable to accept criticism and cannot stand being teased about his ambitions or goals. His feelings are easily hurt.

PERSISTENCE: *Any tie stroke* ≠ ⨍

This person refuses to give up and admit defeat. He may be distracted or detoured from his present plans, but he never loses sight of those plans. He is able to overcome obstacles and will continue fighting until he fulfills his purposes. His motto is: If at first you don't succeed, try, try again. Some persons are persistent to the point of being obstinate. This kind of persistence is annoying to others and causes them to avoid the obstinate individual.

DIGNITY: *Retraced t or d—no loop* ⊥ ⅆ

This person acts according to custom and convention. He seldom gets out of line or defies tradition. He always tries to do the right thing at the right time. He will do the precise things, he will dress carefully, learn what customs and conventions require, and will act accordingly. He is not an individualist.

ENTHUSIASM: *Long, sweeping t-bars* ⊤

He is a lively person who often appears intense and seems to approach all of his interests in life with a great zeal or ardent interest. His enthusiasm is spontaneous and catching. He has the ability to interest others in his projects.

"Fear the Lord, and serve him in truth with all your heart: for consider how great things he hath done for you" (1 Sam. 12:24).

TENACITY: *Final hooks* ᴢ

He holds tightly to whatever he feels is right. Once his mind is made up, it's difficult to change him.

"But that which you have already hold fast till I come" (Rev. 2:25).

IMMATURITY: *The t-bar is inside the stem.* ℓ

He has not yet developed either emotionally or mentally. He may be physically mature, but he is very childish in other ways.

"As newborn babes, desire the sincere milk of the word, that ye may grow thereby" (1 Pet. 2:2).

LAZY: *Separated t-stem with t-bar to left.* $\mathcal{A}$

He is a listless plodder. Laziness has come about through a lack of ambition and drive. He lacks enthusiasm and has no initiative. He often covers this up with a false front.

"[Be] not slothful in business; fervent in spirit; serving the Lord" (Rom. 12:11).

CAUSTIC: *Arrow-like t-bars to right of stem.* λ

His remarks are meant to hurt others. When he wants something done, he has to have it done right away. He often flies off the handle with the slightest provocation, often throwing temper tantrums.

"The merciful man doeth good to his own soul: but he that is cruel troubleth his own flesh" (Prov. 11:17).

SHALLOW: *Basin-like t-bars.* $\mathcal{X}$

This person lacks depth of character and takes a superficial approach to most things in life. He may learn easily, but he lacks serious intent to do his best.

OPTIMISTIC: *Upslant of t-bar* $\mathcal{X}$

He is sure of his ambitions and that he will reach his goals. He has a good outlook on life.

"Therefore, my beloved brethren, be ye steadfast, unmoveable, always abounding in the work of the Lord, forasmuch as ye know that your labour is not in vain in the Lord" (1 Cor. 15:58).

STUBBORN: *Brace structures* ⋏
He blindly refuses to budge, even when he knows he is wrong. He won't listen to reason.
"He, that being often reproved hardeneth his neck, shall suddenly be destroyed, and that without remedy" (Prov. 29:1).

IRRITABILITY or TEMPER: *The t-bar follows the stem.* ⊥
If the t-bar is very light and short, the person is easily irritated. The heavier the stroke the more the temper.
"A man of great wrath shall suffer punishment: for if thou deliver him, yet thou must do it again" (Prov. 19:19).

SARCASTIC: *T-bars are like arrows pointing downward, across, or even slanted upward.* ⤬ ⊥ ⊥
This person makes remarks which cut and hurt others. These sarcastic remarks keep people away from him.

PROCRASTINATION: *T-bars are placed to the left of the stem.* ⊥
This person puts off 'til tomorrow what he should do today. He hesitates in making decisions. This is often caused by a fear of failure or ridicule.
"Behold, now is the accepted time; behold, now is the day of salvation" (2 Cor. 6:2).

WEAK-WILLED: *Very light t-bars.* ⊥
He has little purpose in life and is not sure about what he wishes to accomplish and how to go about it.

STRENGTHENING WILL: *T-bars become heavier at the end.* ⊥
His will becomes stronger with opposition. He reaches high and achieves his goals.
"Finally, my brethren, be strong in the Lord, and in the power of his might" (Eph. 6:10).

MODERATE WILLPOWER: *Medium weight t-bars.* t
    This person has moderate willpower. He sets his own goals and works toward them.

STRONG WILLPOWER: *Heavy t-bars.* t
    He is a forceful individual who sets his own goals. He does this on his own and not by depending on the help of others. He knows what he wants and how to get it.

SELF-CONTROL: *T-bar is bent into a bow.* t
    The will is bent when he has a fault that he wishes to overcome. He has undertaken to get control over some habit or some personal characteristic.
    "Keep yourselves in the love of God, looking for the mercy of our Lord Jesus Christ unto eternal life" (Jude 21).

DELIBERATE: *The upstroke is well separated from the downstroke.* t
    He is slow to move. He takes a lot of time to get things done. He is poky and spiritless.

LOW GOALS: *T-bar sits low on the stem.* t
    He does not make any effort to reach goals and therefore doesn't do very much so far as accomplishments are concerned. He does not believe in his ability to the extent of the fullest capabilities that are present.

PRACTICAL: *T-bar is halfway up the stem.* t
    This person lives from day to day. He does not daydream or make plans far into the future. He is a realist.

HIGH GOALS: *T-bar is three quarters up the stem.* t
    His goals are set far into the future. He is not a daydreamer. The things he plans he makes certain will come to pass.
    "I press toward the mark for the prize of the high calling of God in Christ Jesus" (Phil. 3:14).

LONG-RANGE PLANS: *T-bar sits on top the stem.* 𝒯

He has high ambitions and is able to look far ahead. He has a dream for the future, but he does not lose sight of the present. "Where there is no vision, the people perish" (Prov. 29:18).

DAYDREAMER: *T-bar floats above the stem.* 𝒯̅

Stars are in this person's eyes. He seems to live in the heavenlies and is not realistic about things; therefore he does not see the fruition of his dreams.

RESENTMENT: *Inflexible initial strokes.* 𝒯

He does not like people to make impositions upon him. He is on the defensive and will become indignant when he is pushed too far.

LACK OF DETAILS: *No t-bar.* 𝓵

He doesn't pay attention to details, and therefore he is likely to forget things of importance.

PRIDE IN GOALS: *Tall t-stems but not exaggerated like the vanity stem.* 𝓽

He takes pride in his goals in life and will do his best in anything he undertakes.

SIMPLICITY: *No flourishes or upstrokes. Writing has clean lines.* 𝓽

He doesn't like to waste time. He likes to get to the point quickly.

PRECISION: *Short, well-balanced t-bars.* 𝓽

He is sure to get things done correctly and systematically. He is exacting.

DOMINATING: *Blunt-ended t-bars that are slanted downward.* 𝓧

He has the ability to commmand others to act through the force of his own personality. He is always a leader, not a follower.

DOMINEERING: *Arrow-like t-bars slanted downward.* ↘
He is bossy and always wants his way. He can be overbearing
and mean. This shows his weakness and insecurity.

INDECISIVE: *Weakening finals.* ⟋
He has difficulty in making decisions. He is confused and
uncertain in his thinking and actions.

INDEPENDENT GOALS: *Extremely short t-stems.* ✝
He doesn't go along with the crowd. He makes his own
decisions without the aid of others.

DECISIVE: *Strokes are brought firmly to the base line.* ✝
Being able to make up his mind quickly, his decisions are
easily reached.
"Choose ye this day whom you will serve" (Josh. 24:15).

6
Jane Withers

"We'll name her Jane Withers," said a young mother-to-be one day as she looked up at a theater marquee. "She will bring joy and laughter to many people."

Thus, actress Jane Withers was started on a career even before she was born. Her mother, Ruth Elble Withers, had always wanted to be an actress, but her strict parents disapproved of such a career. Perhaps that is why Ruth dreamed of a movie career for her daughter.

At the age of three, Jane made her professional debut by having her own radio program on an Atlanta station, where she sang and did imitations of W. C. Fields, ZaSu Pitts, Greta Garbo, and Maurice Chevalier. At the memory of it all Jane lowers her eyelids and says, "I was billed as 'Dixie's Dainty Dewdrop.' "

By the time Jane was five she was a big success, and friends and fans urged Mrs. Withers to take her talented daughter to Hollywood. Believing this was the right thing to do, Mrs. Withers gathered together stacks of press clippings and letters of introduction. Then, she and her daughter headed for the theater capital of the world.

"We didn't know one person in that area of the country," says Jane. "The only place Mom knew to go was Hollywood and Vine, the place she'd heard so much about. So she decided, 'I'll get the nearest hotel to Hollywood and Vine so we will be in the right place to make contacts.' But, when she heard what the price was for a hotel there, she knew we could not stay for more than one night. After taking the room, mother went out and bought all the newspapers she could find, hoping to get a reasonably priced apartment the next day."

"Sir, where's the nearest Presbyterian Church?" asked Mrs. Withers of the hotel employee.

"It's only a block from here, lady," he answered, pointing in the direction of the church, "it's on Gower Street."

"Thank you, sir," said Mrs. Withers. Then, turning to her daughter she said, "We'll go there, because that's one place we'll feel at home."

Smiling, Jane recalls, "And we did feel right at home. Doctor Louis Evans, his wife, and the congregation were very gracious to us and we made lots of friends.

"People have told me that it was my impersonation of the rat-tat-tat-tat sound of a machine gun that prompted film director, David Butler, to choose me for the role of "brat" opposite Shirley Temple in "Bright Eyes." I was five years old at the time. When the picture was released, fan mail came pouring in and the press review listed me as a new child sensation."

On her eighth birthday the cameras began rolling on her first starring role in "Ginger," for Twentieth Century-Fox. After forty-seven starring roles and high school graduation, Jane enrolled at UCLA where she planned to major in psychology. This dream was interrupted when America went to war. Putting aside her plans, Jane traveled throughout the United States and Canada making bond and camp tours. In addition to the bond tours, Jane spent every Saturday night at the famous Hollywood Canteen and/or the Stage Door Canteen in New York, making hundreds of records with servicemen which were sent back to their families. Jane still receives letters from friends she made during that time.

Looking back on those years, Jane recalls, "Those were wonderful times. I got to meet everybody and do everything I've ever wanted.

"Faith has played such an important role in my life. I know from my own experiences that faith in God is the real foundation for living, not mere existence. I've always planned things way ahead and would share my thoughts with my parents and with God. I would pray for guidance. In fact, I made many decisions about my future when I was fourteen years old, and as always, I discussed these thoughts with my parents."

Jane's faith was put to the test when illness struck her body. She recalls, "I've always kept an impossible schedule, and in 1953 I suffered a severe attack of rheumatoid arthritis and was completely paralyzed. This was a time of questioning in my life. I thought to myself—*I have done too much, worked too hard, and let my emotions get the better of me.* The X rays, etc., showed definitely that I had arthritis. 'Jane,' the doctor said to me, 'you will be able to get around in a year or two, if things go well.' I had great faith in my doctor and I told him so. But I replied, 'Doctor, God is my partner, and all my life I've put myself in his hands, and with rest and faith I believe I will walk again, and much sooner than you think.' I prayed, silently, 'Lord, I've always needed you, but I'm going to need you now, more than ever. Things have got to move a little faster than maybe they normally would, because I don't have time to waste. My family needs me.' I believed that I would walk again, and much sooner than the doctor has said.

"I spent the time reading many books of inspiration, especially my Bible. My stepfather, Dr. Louis Boonshaft, gave me a copy of Norman Vincent Peale's book, *The Power of Positive Thinking.* Daily, I reaffirmed the thought that I would walk again and believed and trusted God that my body would again be strong and vigorous. And the miracle happened—in nine months I was walking, and there has not been a recurrence.

"In 1963, I decided to go back to work in order to help with the finances. I came to New York to test for the Comet commercial. While I was there I visited with my good friend, Dr.

Peale. As we talked, we both felt that I would be selected for the role of 'Josephine the Plumber'—and I was. There were over one hundred actresses against whom I had to compete. It turned out that we have been the longest running commercial in the history of television." [At the time of this interview the commercials were still being run. JHR]

Dear Joan:

Thank you for your very nice letter of March 11th. and your concern for the health of my mother and the family. At this time we are all fine and have over-come the flu bug and colds.

Many decisions have been made during the past few weeks also, thus the delay in writing to you until now.

I plan to leave for New York on April 3rd. and will film my commercials thru April 10th. If all goes well, I will be free to meet with you on the 11th., 12th. or 13th. for lunch or dinner and a nice visit. I will leave the week-end of the 15th. for Dallas to visit my sons who attend college there and then return to Hollywood for a gala affair at the Century Plaza. I will be honored with an award by the Los Angeles Advertising Women, Inc. for my work in Television commercials. I'll also be a presenter at the same function. This will be April 21st.

I'll be staying at the St. Regis in New York, so please contact me there. They are very good about holding mail and relaying phone messages.

Looking forward to hearing from you when I arrive in New York and of course meeting with you soon.

May God continue to bless you in all that you do.

Most sincerely

Jane Withers

JW/jb

JANE WITHERS

This former child star, known in recent years as "Josephine the Plumber," has an occasional variable slant to her writing. This is expressed by her versatility and sometimes unpredictability and desire for variety. Jane usually will explore all there is to know about something before making any decision on a matter. But, once she makes that decision she sticks to it, that is, unless there is an extremely good reason to change her mind. This she will not hesitate to do if she feels it is necessary. Friendly and outgoing, Jane will do all she can to protect and preserve a friendship and those whom she loves. This bubbly and enthusiastic woman enjoys the attention and affection of others. Miss Withers is a highly intuitive and deeply spiritual person who has keen insight into the unseen world.

7.
Robert H. Schuller

"Jesus Christ was the world's greatest possibility thinker," says Dr. Robert H. Schuller, pastor of Garden Grove Community Church, Garden Grove, California. " 'If you have faith as a grain of mustard seed . . . nothing shall be impossible' " (Matt. 17:20).

"The most powerful motivating force in the world is Christ. When I talk about possibility thinking, I'm not talking about possibility thinking in a humanistic way. The Scripture says, 'I can do all things through Christ which strengtheneth me' (Phil. 4:13). Enthusiasm is energy. It is the fountain of perpetual youth. It is the motivating drive. It literally puts muscles into the body. It becomes the means through which healing and health can come into the body."

Two decades ago, Reverend Robert Schuller and his wife, Arvella, arrived in Orange County, California, with only $500. There they founded a new congregation. Then he negotiated with the owner of a drive-in theater near Disneyland for a temporary center where churchgoers could worship in their automobiles. Finally, he placed messages in the local newspapers inviting area residents to worship at the new center. He made the words, "Come as you are in the family car," a trademark of his ministry.

On March 27, 1955, Robert Schuller preached his first California sermon from the snack bar rooftop at the Orange Drive-In Theater to a congregation of twelve families seated in their automobiles.

The attendance grew and within two years Dr. Schuller and his parishioners moved to their own chapel a few miles away, with the pastor preaching a second service at the theater each Sunday to a drive-in congregation composed of the ill, the elderly, parents with small children, and others who found it difficult to go indoors. Then Schuller decided to combine the best of both services at one location in a simultaneous indoor-outdoor ceremony.

Schuller built his life around the dynamic principle of "Possibility Thinking," a philosophy he has shared with millions of others. It is the subject of many of his televised sermons each year and the basis for his hundreds of books, booklets, and inspirational cassettes.

Robert Schuller was born in Alton, Iowa, in 1926. His missionary uncle predicted that he was destined for the ministry when he was only four years old. Sixteen years later he fulfilled that prediction by entering the Western Theological Seminary of the Reformed Church in America in Holland, Michigan.

His talent for building church congregations became apparent with his first pastoral assignment when membership of his suburban Chicago church increased from 38 to 400 people in four and one-half years. He was subsequently invited to found a West Coast congregation and as a result Garden Grove Community Church was born.

In 1970 Robert Schuller was awarded an honorary doctorate (LL.D.) from Azusa Pacific College and in 1973 was awarded another honorary doctorate (D.D.) from his alma mater, Hope College. Dr. and Mrs. Schuller are the parents of five children.

Says Schuller, "I don't think anybody can be a real possibility thinker unless he understands God like John Calvin did. That meant He is a totally sovereign God. I think Calvin's doctrine of the church was ineffective and inadequate. His doctrine of the church was more negative than it was positive. He said, 'What is a true church? A true church is a church where the

Word is proclaimed, the sacraments administered, and discipline maintained.' All of that, if you analyze it, is a negative reaction. He was reacting against the Roman Catholic Church. He missed the most positive thing.

"My definition of the church is a body of Christ, in community, looking for people who are hurting, and then reaching out through the power of the Holy Spirit and then saying, 'I want to help you. Jesus loves you.'

"It's a very rare thing to find a dynamic, evangelical Christian who is also positive. In my opinion, that is what I find exciting and encouraging in the charismatic movement. Where there is a charismatic movement that is successful, it is positive. We are witnessing today the death of an age in the church. From 1517 to this period of time, if Jesus doesn't come, will be said to have been the reactionary age. We are witnessing today the death of the ecumenical movement and the rebirth of the ecumenical mood. The ecumenical movement which started with the National Council of Churches and the World Council of Churches was institutionalization, and that's what killed it. The movement is virtually dead. But the mood has moved into the charismatic. Ecumenism today is in the charismatic movement, and it's broader and deeper and bigger than anything the National Council of Churches or the World Council of Churches ever envisioned. So what we are witnessing today is the beginning of a new age of church growth. Through the Holy Spirit, Christians are being brought into a oneness, regardless of their church labels. It is church growth based on the love of people for one another, love for the gospel, and put into positive terms.

"The organized ecumenical movement is dead. When an issue becomes an institution which requires executive powers that promise high salaries and ego-status, you've got a problem. When an issue becomes an institution which requires a president, vice-presidents, executive secretaries—that promises good salaries and ego-filling status and power—the movement is in trouble. I believe that the reason why the charismatic movement so far is moving successfully, is because it has not been institutionalized. If it ever is institutionalized and we have an attempt to form an international association of accredited charismatic churches, then we'll have an international president and vice-presidents, those ego-filling labels. They would have to get pretty good salaries and a pretty good international travel expense account. As soon as that happens, the devil is going to move in because there will be human jealousies, human suspicions, and people will be vying for positions by currying favor with one another to get position. It's an observation of a fundamental principle. Jesus always had trouble with the church power people."

But, Dr. Robert Schuller is totally positive as he quotes from Proverbs 3:6, "In everything you do, put God first and he will direct you and crown your efforts with success" (TLB).

I'm so happy our ministry ~~has~~ helped you! / *I LIVE TO HELP PEOPLE!* *The answer to your question is enclosed.* *In His Power,* *Robert Schuller*

ROBERT SCHULLER

Enthusiasm, vim, and vigor help give "possibility-thinking" Dr. Robert Schuller a healthy zest for life. Although he is a dynamic individual who might give the appearance of one who is visionary and possibly extravagant, he basically is an objective, matter-of-fact, down-to-earth person (vertical writing). His goals are within his reach. He is concerned with the present, "what's happening now," as much as he is the future. (Notice the "middle-zone" writing.) The body of the writing is just above the line. Not much extends up or below that "middle-zone." Dr. Schuller likes to get things done efficiently and quickly. He is direct, yet tactful, in his approach to others. Although he enjoys rich color and excitement, his interests and desires are conservative. He is an independent thinker who is cautious in his moves or acceptance of another person or idea. Dr. Schuller has a warm and friendly nature, but he generally expresses his true feeling with moderation.

8.
Troubled Kids

Each child is a personality peculiar to himself. So we must treat him as an individual. Some children have a stronger drive for satisfaction than do other children. Some children withdraw and others are rebellious. Some are retiring.

The child who assumes a belligerent attitude to protect himself against hurt and frustration is the child many people will label as "bad." The child who withdraws himself is likely to go unnoticed. However, this does not make his problem any less. He is more liable to become the kind of person who will break under pressure and become mentally ill.

However, it must not be overlooked that children sometimes find pressure outlets which are socially acceptable. The girl who becomes an accomplished pianist or the boy who becomes a famous athlete might have redirected their need for outlets into these two fine expressions of creativity.

When problems are present in children, they must be viewed in the context of the child's whole life. Of course, we all know how important environment is to anyone. When a child is young, his parents are the central part of his environment. His personality, fears, frustrations, satisfactions, and joys will have a tremendous influence on him and a definite effect on his personality. These early years of a child's life lay the groundwork for his future. Changes are more easily made in his personality during these years than they will be in the years to come.

Most people will readily agree that a well-disciplined child usually will respond to the wishes of his parents and other adults. Of course, we know that the demands of adults on a child should be made for the child's well-being, and not merely to accommodate the adults. A child feels more secure if he is made to obey by those who love and understand him.

We can apply the same rules when we analyze a child's handwriting as when we analyze an adult's. However, we need to realize that irregularity and unsteadiness of strokes are characteristics of a child's writing. When he acquires some degree of skill in writing, the speed increases and regularity begins to improve. Just as the handwritings of adults deviate from the school pattern, likewise do the handwritings of children.

An adult who can readily withstand frustrations usually had a satisfying infancy and childhood. No one setback ever causes a mental breakdown. When an adult gives way in the face of misfortune, it is because he still carries with him unhealed emotional scars from an earlier time in his life. The incident which seemingly causes the breakdown is only the door that reopens the wound.

Psychologists and counselors who work with adolescents who steal, lie, or play truant often remark that there are more problem parents than problem adolescents. In effect, the unresolved emotional conflicts in parents are often the root of the problem behavior exhibited by the adolescents. More and more it is believed that those persons who know most about the physical, emotional, and mental growth of children are those parents and teachers who are themselves well-adjusted and well-integrated. Children learn by our example. They do not inherit mental instability from their parents. The normal development of children is jeopardized by parents who are unstable. Personality integration is a basic essential in parents and teachers if they are to do their best on behalf of the children who are under their care.

Almost all criminal tendencies in teenagers where sex crimes are committed are traceable to some form of misconception about sex. So it is of prime importance that children be given the best example at home, where love and understanding will direct them into a successful life. Parents should treat the subject of sex exactly as they treat any other topic, being sure to give the adolescent answers to his questions as he can understand them. This is a good way to keep youth from being obsessed with sex, and they will feel that they can come to their parents with any more questions about the subject. Teenagers take their problems to someone they know, like, and respect.

A teenager is a person in transition. He is leaving childhood and approaching adulthood. Even though he has not had much experience, he responds to a challenge. He craves activity and he is happiest when he exercises self-control.

A well-known medical man told me the story of how he helped a certain mother and child. The mother had a son who was in high school. Harold's grades were low and sometimes not even passing. His mother was worried and this affected her own health.

Finally, the doctor suggested that she provide him with a sample of the youth's handwriting. He thought this might give him the answer. It did. The handwriting revealed that the boy was so self-conscious that he was afraid to stand up in front of the class at school. He knew the answers, but he thought the other classmates knew so much more than he did. And between underrating his own ability and the self-consciousness, he was making his high school days agony, not only for himself but for his mother and teachers, too.

This doctor often uses handwriting analysis in his search to understand his patients. He showed the boy from the boy's own handwriting that he was just as bright and maybe brighter mentally than some of his classmates. The doctor convinced the young man that there was no reason why he should be self-conscious or have fears. He then explained to the mother how to work with the boy to help him in oral class preparation. When the boy discovered for himself that he knew, and was able to hold his own with his classmates, he solved his problem. His grades went higher and his mother's health improved.

Bill

The following is the true account of a teenager who did not get the needed emotional and spiritual help that was indicated in his handwriting. The result was tragic.

Bill was just sixteen years old the night he walked into the church with his friend, David. He had never been in a church before and his mother and father had warned him when he asked if he could go that he'd better not get religious. "They're all hypocrites," his dad had warned him. But these people seemed to be so happy. They greeted him with so much enthusiasm that he felt like they really cared about him.

Bill had never seen so many young people near a church as he saw this night. David had called it a renewal meeting, or something like that. Whatever it was called didn't matter to Bill, because when they had sat down and the minister of music led the congregation in singing he couldn't believe his ears. As he looked about the room he saw those same kids that had greeted him so warmly singing and clapping their hands like they were having a great time.

Later on, a young minister got up and talked right to the people. The things he said seemed to make a lot of sense to Bill, even though he had never heard anything like this before. He drank in every word the minister said. "If you want real joy and peace in your life, try Jesus. Perhaps you've tried the things of the world and found that they don't give real satisfaction and peace. If you have found that the world doesn't offer that which you are looking for, I say again, try Jesus."

"Boy," thought Bill, "I've sure tried everything; cigarettes, liquor, drugs, girls, everything, and I know they don't really satisfy. Maybe this man is right. I've never seen people as happy as these people seem to be."

The minister went on, "If you want this peace and joy that doesn't past away, I say again, try Jesus. Get out of your seat and walk to the front where I am standing, thus signifying that you wish to know the Savior's love in your own life."

Bill watched as many teenagers and others got up out of their seats and hurried to the front of the church. A few tears filled the corners of his eyes as he sat there. But he didn't get out of his seat. He didn't move from the spot where he was sitting.

When all those who were going to come were standing at the front of the church, the pastor talked with them briefly and then directed them to a prayer room to the front side of the sanctuary.

Later, as Bill and David were walking from the church, Bill broke out with, "I wanted to come. I really did, but Mom and Dad would be angry if I got religious. They said so before I came tonight. Mom and Dad hate religion. They both went to church when they were kids but Dad says all the people in the church are hypocrites, and he doesn't want any part of it and I can't get involved with it either."

David interrupted with "But, Bill, we shouldn't let other people affect our lives like that. We should follow Jesus and his teachings, and not the people of the churches. They are human just like us, and can make mistakes. You're not perfect just because you're a Christian. By God's help we live from day to day, and if we make a mistake and ask his forgiveness he will forgive us."

"I really dig Jesus. What that preacher said about him makes me think that he's a regular guy. He sounds like someone that I'd like to get to know. But Dad would really be mad if I got on another 'kick.' "

"You don't have to go up in front of a church to become a Christian. You can talk with Christ wherever you are."

"Maybe I'll do that one of these days. I'll think about it."

Things seemed to go from bad to worse for Bill. When he told his parents about the religious meeting, they reminded him that he'd better not go to that church again. They didn't want a religious fanatic in the family. So, Bill, not wanting to cause any more disturbances in the family, tried to forget about that night when he went with David to the "renewal meeting." But he couldn't forget it. He kept hearing, over and over again in his mind, the words the preacher spoke that night, about how we can be forgiven of our sins by putting our trust in this man called Jesus. Bill continued on his "merry-go-round" of sin and became more and more despondent.

The Kinards lived a few blocks from Bill and his family. They were planning a vacation and asked Bill to come by every day to feed their dog and take in the mail. He'd taken care of the dog once before when the Kinards went away. Besides, he didn't have a dog and had always enjoyed playing with their dog, Rover.

It was the week of June 7. Bill and his friends had gone swimming after school. It would be only a few more days until school would be over for the year, so there was not much homework to do. Anyhow, Bill's grades weren't going to be good. He'd lost interest in his studies, in fact he didn't care much about anything anymore. "Life doesn't seem worth living," thought Bill as he and his friends dived for the last time before leaving for home.

The boys dried off with their towels, rolled them up, and put them in the baskets of their bikes and took off for home as if they were in a big race. It was time for dinner and the swimming had made them hungry.

When they reached Bill's house, he hopped off his bike and

said, "Good-bye, fellas. This'll be the last time I'll be going swimming."

The boys said good-bye as they raced on down the road, with Terry doing one of his usual "wheelies." (Pulling up on the handlebars of a bicycle and thus causing the front wheel to raise up off the ground.) Terry thought a minute and then said, "Wonder what he meant by that? (meaning the last time I'll be going swimming). Guess he's going on vacation."

A few days later Bill skipped school and went downtown to the bank. He drew out all the money from his savings account and asked to have it put into his parents' account. Had he asked to have the money himself, instead of putting it into his parents' account, the bank officers undoubtedly would have been a little reluctant to go along with his request to withdraw the money. Bill took the cancelled bankbook and stuffed it in his pocket, then hurried out of the bank. That evening he asked a friend to take over the responsibility of the care of the dog. He took the friend over to the Kinard home and unlocked the door. He had told his friend that he might be called out of town for a few days and that was why he needed a substitute for the job.

"He's a good dog. As long as you feed him and let him run outside every day he'll be all right."

"OK," promised his friend, "I'll take good care of him. Don't worry about it."

The next day, after his brothers and sisters had left home to go to school and his parents had gone to their jobs, Bill went up to his bedroom and got out his writing paper. He picked up a pen and began to write. When he had finished writing, he signed his name and folded the note. Then he wrote the names on the top of the folded paper: "Mom and Dad." He took a second piece of paper and began writing again. This note was addressed to Mr. and Mrs. Kinard. Bill took the note which he addressed to his mom and dad and put it on the dresser in their bedroom. Then he stuffed the other note in his pocket and went downstairs and out the door, looking back longingly as he went. His mind was in a turmoil and his heart was thumping wildly.

Down the street and up to the Kinard's door he went, unlocking it quickly and hurrying inside. He made his way to the basement and got everything ready. Next he ran upstairs and pulling the note out of his pocket laid it next to the telephone. Frantically, he looked up the telephone number of the local police and dialed the number.

"Hello," he blurted out breathlessly, "is this the police?"

"Yes," answered the low-voiced police officer, "what is it?"

"I wanted to tell you to come over to 44 North Melburn Street. Go to the basement when you get there!" said the young voice on the other end of the line.

"Who is this? What's your name?" asked the officer, his voice becoming increasingly tense. "Who is this?"

Click, went the receiver on this end. Bill had placed the phone back on the hook.

A short time later the sound of a police siren came closer and closer to the Kinard house. As the patrol car stopped two policemen jumped out and ran up the steps to the house. They rang the bell quickly, and not waiting for an answer rushed into the house and down to the basement. The first policeman to get to the bottom of the steps stopped suddenly.

"Ohhhh," he moaned. "We're too late. Look over there," he said as he pointed to the back section of the basement.

The two officers stood back startled and then rushed over to where the boy was. One of the officers cut the rope. But it was too late.

"Why would a young boy do a thing like this?" asked one of the men.

"Why? Why?"

So often we ask ourselves why, but many times it is too late. Too late for a boy like this to be helped.

When Bill had gone to the church with David a few months before, his heart was searching for the reality of Christ. No one knew the turmoil that lay in his mind and heart. If only his parents had realized their son's spiritual need, as well as their own spiritual need. They had called the people of the church hypocrites, but they never stopped to realize that the church is one of the places for hypocritical and sinful people to find strength to make changes in the way they are living. Had Bill been able to freely come to the church and accept Christ as his Savior, as he had wanted to do, the pastor could have counseled with him and made an effort to help him by praying with him and teaching him the Word of God.

Had I been given a sample of Bill's handwriting I would have seen the terribly sensitive nature, indicated by the erratic slant of his writing.

Of course by the time I was given Bill's handwriting for analysis it was too late. If only I'd seen it before, I say. Perhaps the enlightenment brought about by the report could have been the means to save his life. No one knows. Let us look at a copy of the two notes left by Bill. It should tell us a lot about the boy's problem.

Bill's Handwriting

Bill's handwriting lacked consistency and emotional stability. Notice the variable slant of the writing. Some letters are vertical, some have the backhand slant, while others have the far forward slant. We must, however, make some allowance for the fact that Bill was at the age of puberty. He was at the age of struggle between childhood and maturity.

Having a keen imagination along the lines of spiritual things, Bill let his imaginative mind run away with him. Look at the wide upper loops of the h and look at the word *Thanks* in the top letter. There is an a made with invasions into the inside of the circles indicating that he was not always honest with himself or with others. There are many other evidences of traits such as yieldingness, stubbornness, and shallowness, but let us look finally at the signature in both cases. Notice the way the letters seem to grow and fly away.

The Lesbian

Most parents are concerned about the growth and maturity of their children. Another important concern is that the children develop into normal and socially acceptable individuals. The peer group is very influential upon a child's future. Thus it is vital that he or she associate with the kind of friends who will be an influence in the right direction.

The following is the account of one teenager who got herself involved in a questionable relationship, and how both mother and daughter found a way out.

"I have a problem, a personal problem concerning my daughter," said a woman who identified herself as Mrs. Filor as she talked with me on the phone one day. "I heard you speak on the science of handwriting analysis at the Englewood Christian Women's Club several months ago and I would like to have my daughter's handwriting analyzed.

"Betty is only fourteen years old and has become very close friends with an unsaved girl who is known to be a Lesbian. My daughter seems to be led by this girl's strong personality and has lost the desire to go to church and to enjoy friendships among the church youth. Her school grades have dropped and there is little communication between us. She won't confide in me as she used to do."

"Do you have any idea what the cause of the problem might be?" I asked.

"Well, no, not really. It all started about the time that her sister Gloria received a coveted scholarship for college. Gloria is such a bright girl, who brings her father and me nothing but pleasure. She and I have always been so close. I keep telling Betty that she should try to be more like her sister and get good grades. It doesn't seem to make any difference to her, though."

"Have you always used Gloria as an example to Betty?"

"I don't think I have; well, maybe a little, now and then."

"Encouraging Betty to follow in her sister's footsteps might be a part of the problem. Maybe she feels that she can't or doesn't want to follow in her sister's footsteps. If you will bring me several pages of Betty's writing, preferably on unlined paper, and a copy of her signature I will do what I can to give you a true analysis of your daughter's writing," I said.

"Oh, yes, I will. I'll get it for you this coming week."

Mrs. Filor went on to tell me about the kind of home that the Lesbian girl came from and how there was no parental control over the children. "Whatever the children want to do they are permitted to do. They call it a part of the 'free society.' " But this story is nothing new. Too many parents today do not believe in restraining their children or giving them guidance. "Let them find their own way. Let them decide when they grow up if they want to attend church and be a Christian or not."

A few days later there was a knock on my door. It was Mrs. Filor.

"Hello, Mrs. Filor," I said. "Come in."

"I want to tell you that there is no improvement where Betty is concerned. She is getting more rebellious than ever. Here are the handwriting samples that you asked for. I found several pages of notes from her schoolwork and here is a copy of her signature."

"Good, I shall let you know my findings as soon as I can. The analysis is sure to help us get to the root of her problems. Now, I think it would be a good idea if we asked God's help in the matter."

After a brief moment of prayer Mrs. Filor went on her way.

It did not take long to find a few clues to Betty's difficulty. It was pretty much as I had expected. Betty had given up in the competition with her sister, Gloria, for her mother's admiration. Being a child with a personality different from her sister, Gloria, Betty did not possess the aptitude for learning science, mathematics, and like subjects as did her sister. It was more difficult for Betty to comprehend. Gloria was able to grasp the knowledge of a subject so much faster. But there was one thing which I found about Betty's abilities. She possessed a talent for the arts. If it were developed, she might be able to become an artist in one of the related fields. She possessed a certain amount of rhythm, balance, and control in her writing; an invaluable asset to an artist. But Betty was not a leader, and a very serious problem was that she did not have much drive or many goals set for herself. Nearly all of her t-bars were crossed low on the stems, indicating a lack of goals and ambition. Also, the direction of the body of her writing slanted downhill, indicating pessimism and depression. Betty was satisfied to let things be as they were. The battle of competition with her sister was too much for her. This made her fair prey for unhealthy relationships like that with the Lesbian.

A few days later I received a call from Mrs. Filor wanting to find out the report of the analysis. "I think I've gotten some insight into Betty's problems," I said. "Can you come by this afternoon?"

"Yes, certainly, I have been so eager to know what the results of the analysis would be."

When Mrs. Filor arrived, I explained to her the basic personality of her daughter and the problems as they were revealed in the writing. I also encouraged her not to use sister Gloria as an example to Betty, but to encourage Betty as an individual to develop her own talents, especially along the line of the arts, where she had obvious talent.

"Make it possible for Betty to take art lessons," I told her, "and give her encouragement in pursuing the training."

"Oh, I will," she promised. "I do remember Betty talking about having an interest in painting and drawing, but I never did much to encourage her in doing anything about it. I guess I've been too preoccupied with the success of my other daughter, Gloria."

"Quite likely," I agreed. "Let me see another sample of Betty's writing in a month or so. Keep her as busy as possible with activities that interest her and will bring you two closer. This might help take her attention away from that girl."

Sure enough. The next month when Mrs. Filor brought the handwriting sample to me there was a marked change. The t-bars were crossed at a higher point, there was more control to the basic structure of the writing, and the body of the writing did not have the same downhill slant as it had had before.

"Betty loves her art lessons," said Mrs. Filor, "and she is beginning to talk with me more and confide in me. Also, I never mention Gloria's achievements in front of Betty."

Mrs. Filor was cooperative and made such a change in her relationship with her daughter that a few months later, when I received a third specimen of Betty's writing the t-bars were higher still, and there was much more control and ambition in the writing. In fact, the direction of the body of the writing was beginning to go uphill.

"My daughter and I are so close now," remarked Mrs. Filor on her last visit to my office, "and she is no longer close friends with the Lesbian girl. Instead, she is too involved in her art work and youth activities at the church. She has made a new dedication to God."

9.
The Humbards

REX HUMBARD

"I used to wear blue jeans to play and sing on my radio show back in Arkansas, 'cause blue jeans was all I had to wear; and some of them were pretty threadbare," says Rex Humbard, the "homespun" preacher from Akron, Ohio.

Humbard's television and shortwave radio programs reach as many as 100 million persons each week in areas of six continents where half the world's population lives. Originating mostly from the Cathedral of Tomorrow, his television programs (as of 1978) are carried on more than 550 television stations and more than 1,000 satellite stations.

For Humbard, the marble and glass cathedral symbolizes his dream and mission in life—to help people find answers to their problems, but especially to reach the world with "the gospel." "In the past I've worshiped God under the shade of a tree, on the platform of a truck, in a brush arbor, in a tent, and a ragged tent at that."

In his down-to-earth manner, Humbard explains, "It doesn't matter whether I'm in a little auditorium, or a big auditorium, I act the same way. I shake hands with the people as long as they are waiting for me. I know that the next Sunday when I appear on TV I'm not preaching 'on the largest network in the world.' I'm preaching to individuals. They are the ones who are on my mind. They write me or tell me in person how much the program means to them—the people who are sick and in wheelchairs, or depressed and unhappy. And that does something to me. They say, 'Please pray for me.' Everybody is looking for someone who can help him find the answer to his problem. The next Sunday, after I hear of these needs I, when I preach, subconsciously know who is at home listening to me."

Humbard believes religion should be universal, and dividing it into sects has contributed to its decline. The congregation of the Cathedral of Tomorrow is comprised of many denominations. A firm of Jewish architects designed the cathedral complex at no cost. He says, "As my father once said, 'The church doesn't belong to any denomination. There is only God's family and the devil's family.' "

Rex was born on August 13, 1919, in Hot Springs, Arkansas. The oldest of six children, Rex Emmanuel Humbard never attended a seminary and was ordained by his father, an itinerant preacher who, likewise, never attended a seminary. Rex's mother and father spent their time traveling the continent, singing and preaching and playing a large variety of musical instruments. Rex, himself, soon became known for his gospel guitar music.

"When I was thirteen in Hot Springs, Arkansas," he recalls, "I watched the Ringling Brothers' Circus come to town." I said, "If God had a tent like that, he'd have a crowd like that. God ought to be on Main Street."

Rex Humbard got his tent—a "Gospel Big Top" circus tent that had a portable stage and seated 6,000 people. Gradually, a radio audience was built, first on local stations and then on the Mutual Broadcasting System network.

In Indianapolis, in 1942, after a Sunday night service at Cadle Tabernacle, Rex married Maude Aimee Jones, a singer he'd met when the Humbard family went to Dallas, Texas. The ceremony was witnessed by over eighty-five hundred persons.

Traveling in a trailer or battered bus or car, Humbard set up his gospel tent wherever he felt God leading him. In 1952, the

"Gospel Big Top" came to Akron, Ohio. Crowds were so great that twice as many people had to be turned away nightly as could be accommodated in the tent which seated 6,000. When the tent finally moved on to Cleveland, many of the Akron audience followed. This led to Rex's decision to stay in that area. With only sixty-five dollars in his pocket, he decided to build a "work" in Akron, in the old Copley Theater. Later, he moved to a onetime theater on State Road in Cuyahoga Falls, Ohio, in 1953. He renamed the theater Calvary Temple. Plans were laid for erecting a church at Portage Trail and State Road, the site of the present cathedral.

In 1957, acting as his own contractor, Humbard began building the circular edifice with its five thousand theater seats. The cathedral was completed in 1958, on a portion of the fourteen and one-half acres the cathedral owns.

In 1971, construction was completed on the cathedral apartments, a $2.5 million, thirteen-story building for the elderly, Federally financed and sponsored by the church.

For more than twenty-five years Rex Humbard has appeared regularly on his own TV program with the services tailored for TV. Dressed in inexpensive but stylish suits, Humbard looks like an influential businessman. Says Humbard, "Years ago, everybody thought I was a millionaire. Actually, as long as the organization suffered, I suffered. Many times down through the years we had to take a tire out of the trunk of our car to sell for food or clothing or a mortgage."

For many years the Humbards lived in a very modest home across the street from the Cathedral of Tomorrow. Then a wealthy woman died. In her estate was her large house in a highly desirable part of Akron. To close the estate, the house was offered for sale by secret bids. The Cathedral of Tomorrow made a very modest bid, which has never been made public but which was far below the value of the property, and the Cathedral's bid was accepted. The house became the parsonage for the church and home for the Humbards.

However, the house, and some of the other endeavors of the church, caused some to criticize the Humbards for making "big business" out of religion and "living in luxury." To those critics, Humbard responds, "I don't own a home. I don't own a car. The organization, the Cathedral of Tomorrow, owns the home. The home was bought to entertain people like Oral Roberts, Pat Boone, Kathryn Kuhlman—people like that. It's easier to get to know someone when they sit at your table and dine with you than it is to just sit in an auditorium with them. But I could live anywhere. I don't think God looks at what you have. It's what you do with what you have that counts. We love the home, but I could move out into a tent tomorrow and I'd still preach."

REX HUMBARD

A lover of responsibility (full R in Rex; H in Humbard), Rex is individualistic and always full of new ideas. He is apt to do the unexpected. It is difficult to predict his next move. (Variable slant in writing. The body of the writing doesn't stay on the "imaginary" base line.) Once he has made up his mind to do something he will push ahead toward his objective. A spiritual, though practical man, Rex is extremely sensitive and, at times, very emotionally expressive. (Look at the wide-looped d in Humbard. The wider the loop the more sensitive the person.) This TV, country-boy preacher loves ceremony and fanfare. Persistent and self-confident, he is a self-made man.

ELIZABETH HUMBARD

"I believe my musical talent is a gift from God and is to be used for him," says cute, blond-haired, eighteen-year-old Liz Humbard, daughter of TV preacher, Rex Humbard.

"My friend, singing star Connie Smith, inspired me to start to sing. At first I tried her style, but as time went on she showed me how to 'feel my music out,' do my own thing, the style which was most comfortable for me. Now it is completely changed from when I first started singing.

"So far as the 'rock beat' is concerned, I think that if you use a hymn that kids aren't familiar with you might not reach them. The rock beat will stick in their minds where another type of song won't. I sing a song called, 'I Can't Stop Loving Him,' which has the kind of beat that will keep rolling around in their minds and at the same time they think of the words to the song.

"Don't get me wrong. The old-time hymns of the church are great. I don't know all of them, but I love the ones I do know.

"I used to dislike being a preacher's kid. That is, until October 27, 1974, when I really and sincerely gave my heart to the Lord. Now I'm happy about it.

"You hear a lot about kids who aren't saved—the riotous kids. Some people say everything is wrong with the teenage world—this generation. But there are a lot of kids who are turning on to Jesus, and are real excited about it—more so than some adults. Jesus is becoming a main topic of their conversations. It's wonderful how the subject of Jesus is coming up in everyday life. Satan really tries to get down on the Christian kids because people look at them to be different from other kids. This is where being a minister's kid is a big responsibility. People will look at the minister and say, 'If he can't control his own family, he must not be what he says he is.' Those are the kids that people are really going to pick on.

"Sometimes as a result of teasing, a young person will rebel from something he or she really loves and wants. Teasing used to bug me, but now I have something to fall back on. I know what I've got is real, so teasing doesn't faze me anymore.

"I've always been a daddy's girl. Most girls are. If I have a problem, like where I am dealing with the Scripture and I can't understand something, I'll usually go to Daddy. Of course, if I want to talk about something pertaining to girls, I'll go to mother.

"I want to marry somebody like Daddy—somebody who loves you for what you are and is willing to work with you and you work with him. I think it is important to a marriage that the two people have a common interest and common goal. It's important that you both are Christians and that what you do is the will of God. I'm not worried about who I'll marry because I know God has the right man for me.

"Concerning the subject of sex, I think that's one subject many kids today are getting hung up on. Some say sex before marriage is OK so long as you don't go the whole way. But I think that this is the wrong attitude. We should have a set of moral values, guidelines, by which we live. If kids get involved in sex before marriage, they will miss a whole lot. Sex is something beautiful to those who are married and if they experience it ahead of time, they will lose the appreciation for marriage. The Bible says it is sinful for a man and woman out of the holy bond of marriage to touch one another's bodies. I believe that's the way it is."

ELIZABETH HUMBARD

An obedient and rather shy girl who seems older than her years, Liz Humbard is likely to appreciate the experience and advice she is given by her parents and other elders. She has lots of intuition and an appreciation for the spiritual. She has good powers of concentration and self-control. (Notice the small, well-balanced, well-formed letters.) Warm and friendly, Liz likes it when people notice her and give her the assurance that she is doing her job well. This is sufficient for her to go on. She doesn't need a lot of "show-biz" type of vainglory. With her gentle sort of way she is more likely to be a follower than a leader. She would make a good cooperator in almost any type of venture—such as business or that of marriage. She possesses a good sense of rhythm and musical ability which is exhibited when she appears on her father's television program each week. A sweet girl.

10.
Look Up, Look Down

Handwriting is divided into three zones. The upper, middle, and lower zones. The upper zone, including the upper loops of the small letters b-h-l-k and f, reveals some form of imagination present in the writing. The size of the loop reveals the amount of imagination that is present. The t and d are the only exceptions to this rule. Imagination is the ability of the mind to form mental images of ideas or objects not present to the senses.

When the upper loops in a writing are very high or tall it indicates spiritual or philosophical thinking. *(handwriting sample)*

The middle zone of writing reveals the realm of the soul and also the functioning of the personality, expression, ego, and social relationships. The middle zone letters are a-c-e-i-m-n-o-r-s-u-v-w and x. It is the social zone; the practical and daily life.

The lower zone, or the loops below the line, are indicative of material imagination. It is the realm of the instincts, the biological and sex drives, and the material drives and desires. There are seven lower loop letters in our alphabet: f-g-j-p-q-y and z. Long lower loops reveal a desire for variety and change. This writer wants a change in his life. It may be a vacation. It may be that he wants a job where he is able to move about or has a change in the daily work. The need for variety is measured by the size of the loop in relation to the overall size of the writing.

(handwriting sample)

Lower loops which are small and squared show clannishness. This writer likes a restricted group of friends. It may include one, two, or three close associates. He may make friends easily but he does not include his acquaintances in his confidence. He may be considered a good mixer, but there will always be that underlying policy of limiting trusted friends.

Very slender lower loops in the y-j or g indicates a careful selection of friends.

Writers of lower loops that are not completed and the stroke swings to the left, have imagination that is undeveloped; that lacks direction.
They imagine, but they do not make any effort to carry out these imaginations.

REVIEWING WHAT WE HAVE JUST LEARNED:

(1) A large lower loop reveals imagination.
(2) The size of the loop indicates the activity of the imagination.
(3) A stroke that swings to the left and is not completed shows imagination that is unused or undirected.
(4) The length of the loops reveals the desire a person has for change.

When the loops of one line of writing run into the line below, the writer has too many interests and the result is confusion.

Another lower loop that has a distinct meaning of its own is found in the lowercase p. It can be long, slender, with a large loop, or without much loop. It may have a stem instead of a lower loop.

When the letter *p* has a large loop, the writer has highly developed physical mindedness, the desire for physical activity. This does not mean that the writer is physically active because there are conditions where a person's mental desire cannot be supported by physical response. For example, a person with a serious physical handicap like heart disease, arthritis, or no use of his arms or legs, may still show the desire for physical activity, even though he cannot carry out those desires. In chapter 1 I said "handwriting is brain-writing." If this is true, then you can understand how handwriting is a picture of mental, not physical habits. If there is a physical handicap, then we see how there cannot be physical reaction, even though the mental desire is still there.

The lower zone reveals a person's biological drives, their degree of sensuality, and frustration of, or abstinence from erotic drives (love desires). An exaggeration in size of the lower loops, in comparison to the middle and upper zones, indicates a strong interest in the material world and the world of instincts.

Joan - Alfred

UPPER LOOPS

Egotist: *Capital I out of proportion to the script.*
 This person is conceited, self-centered, and overly prowd of himself. He is often narrow-minded and bigoted. He demands attention when it is not deserved.
Practical Philosophy: *Short, narrow loops:*
 He has a down-to-earth philosophy of life. He is not interested in theories, because, for him these are impractical. He takes everything at face value.
Restricted Philosophy: *Tall, narrow loops.*
 He will suffer much guilt and self-condemnation from his

limited beliefs. His code of ethics is extremely restricted, and he cannot accept new concepts.

Philosophical: *Tall, wide loops.*

This person has very high ideals in life. He seldom sees things as they really are.

Responsibility: *Capitals have wide, rounded loops.*

This person loves to take on responsibilities. He is willing to carry the big load on a job. He is a very dependable person.

Broad-mindedness: *Fat, well-rounded e's and flat topped r's.*

He has an open mind and is extremely tolerant of the viewpoints of others. He is an understanding individual.

Narrow-mindedness: *Cramped or restricted e's.*

He is not interested in the viewpoints of others, unless they happen to agree with his own. He is unable to see more than one side of any issue. He will close his mind and automatically reject new theories.

Warped: *Wavy or dented loops.*

He is extremely distorted in his viewpoints on everything, and is very eccentric. He is mentally unstable.

LOWER LOOPS

Clannish: *Restricted loops on end of the downstroke.*

He is a loner, and when he does socialize, it is always with a small group of people.

Physical Activity: *Loop on small p.*

This person craves physical activity and action.

Imaginative: *Inflated loops.*

He has an active imagination, and adds originality and individuality to everything he does.

Selectivity: *Slender loops, not returning to the base line.*

Although he is not unfriendly, he is very selective in choosing the few who really ever get to know him well. He prefers small groups rather than crowds.

Restrictive Imagination: *Extremely slender loops.*

It is difficult for him to visualize things. When he presents an idea, he will be factual and never exaggerate things.

Love of Variety: *Long loops run down but do not intermingle with the upper loops of the line below.*

He loves variety and change in his life. He doesn't like being confined to any routine, and becomes restless when tied down for a long period of time. He enjoys travel and has a variety of interests.

Confusion: *Intermingling of upper and lower loops.*

He always has too many irons in the fire. He ends up confused, and with a feeling of frustration. Although he already carries more than a full load, he continually adds more.

11.
Betsy Palmer

"People I work with ask if I found God when I went to a Billy Graham Crusade," says Betsy Palmer, well-known TV and stage star." I answer, 'Yes, as a matter of fact, I did.' But I don't think they believe me."

Blonde Betsy Palmer won the hearts of TV viewers when she was seen on programs like "What's My Line," "Philco Playhouse," "Studio One," and "Playhouse 90." Greater popularity came from her appearance on the "I've Got a Secret" show and her own show, "Girl Talk."

Broadway shows like *South Pacific, Cactus Flower,* and *The Prime of Miss Jean Brodie* made the same Betsy Palmer almost a legend.

Always interested in people and their lives, this "girl next door" will remember things about those she meets, even to the smallest detail. Says Betsy, "As a little girl, I never went to church. My parents always said it was up to my brother and me to choose whatever we wanted to do in that area of our lives when we got to the age to make that decision. But I never made that decision, completely. However, I remember when I was about eleven years old a very religious lady, who was a family friend, showed me something about Christianity that I'd never known before. I can remember taking communion with her in a Baptist church. All through my life I was touched by truly Christian people, but never to the point where I myself took the step. I even sang in the choir of the Methodist church in my hometown, but I never really understood what it meant to be a Christian.

Betsy didn't plan to be an actress. After graduating from high school, she attended her mother's business college for six months. Then she worked for a year and a half as a stenographer for the local railroad company. After a year of this, Betsy's parents suggested she further her education. An aptitude test at the local YWCA showed she had a propensity for dealing with people in interpersonal relationships and a flair for the arts. Since she liked acting, she chose to major in it at DePaul University. After graduation from college she decided that New York should be her next step. That was in 1951. Soon she was on her way to a successful career as an actress.

"God's hand has been on my life from the very beginning, but I don't think I ever realized it. I used to call it 'good luck,' but now I know that God working within you, within your mind, within your heart, within the very essence of you—your soul—prepares you for the things which will happen to you."

Little did Betsy realize that God's choice of her chauffeur would be a minister of the gospel. This was in 1963 when she was performing at the Paper Mill Playhouse in New Jersey.

Reverend David Shepson's wife had been seriously injured in a fire. He was forced to get additional income to pay hospital and doctor bills. This is why he began working part-time for a driving school. His having a chauffeur's license was one reason why he was asked to take the job with Betsy. Shepson accepted the job, realizing the opportunity he would have to witness to her for Christ.

"We have had such marvelous talks," mused Betsy. "He has enlightened me about the Scriptures and has answered questions that I had wanted to ask for years."

Shepson recalls, "I remember that one year I drove Betsy to her various theatrical performances more than 100 nights. If a limousine wouldn't be available, she'd be very willing to accept a ride in my own station wagon. In fact, she never wanted to be treated like a celebrity, often sitting right up in front with the driver. Sometimes we'd sing as we rode along. Other times she would be deep in thought, or just resting. I only spoke when I was spoken to. I took every opportunity to talk about Christ."

He continued, "Betsy always thought highly of Christ and believed that he had been a great and wonderful man. She thought she knew him in a way, but now she realized that without the 'new birth' she could not really know him."

About this time, Betsy became an active worker with the Salvation Army. She admits, "I've found I can't say no when these people ask me to do something. They are wonderful human beings—not only the people in the Army, but also those I have met through the Army; big bankers, people who are wealthy, and people who are not wealthy."

But Betsy's search for a vital spiritual experience continued. "I was afraid of religion. I was afraid I would have to be a part of 'organized religion.' "

"I'm going to quit running," she told her mother at the beginning of the summer of 1970. "I'm not going to do any summer stock."

So, when Betsy received an invitation to go along to a Billy Graham Crusade, she said yes.

"It was pleasant to sit and listen to the whole program," recalls Betsy, "but I think I especially enjoyed watching the thousands of people who were there—the young people—the singing—then, of course, when Dr. Graham got up and spoke. He's such an awesome man. He is a very thought-provoking man who has tremendous charisma. I think any of us who have charisma, and people tell me that I have it, I believe that it is God-given. It is for us to take and choose whichever path we want to go with it—that turns it good or bad.

"As I was sitting there in Shea Stadium watching people

Betsy Palmer

Darling Joan -
This was sent
to me by mistake.
- Thank you for
coming with us
and also for doing
your show for the
Rotary - They
said you were
enchanting -

Love

Betsy

BETSY PALMER

walk down the aisles, the thought never went through my mind that I would walk to the front. And it would not have happened unless my friend, Joan Robie, had said, 'Don't you think you'd like to go to the front?'

"As we went down onto the field, I felt like I was in another world. It was a very strange kind of light-headed, happy feeling. I can only liken it to 'opening night butterflies' because my heart was beating faster and faster. I suppose the medical profession could describe it as having palpitations, or something like that. It didn't make any difference whether I could hear Billy Graham's words or not. I felt overwhelmed, safe, and really kind of very new.

"All I know is that God has given me something since that time that I didn't have before. I know he is going to take care of me, no matter what the predicament might seem. In fact, I have since that time had a few things happen to me that I don't understand. And yet, I know God is preparing me to do good, his good, by being able to reach out and touch people and help them."

Just as she appears on television, Betsy Palmer is a warm, friendly, and intuitive person (breaks between letters show intuition). A lover of responsibility, Betsy has lots of physical energy, and carries out the long-range plans she makes. (Long, lower loops, such as those on the letter y reveal her physical drive. The T-bar crossed at the top of the T-stem.) Although she is somewhat of a "free spirit" and very enthusiastic (notice long T-bar on the name, Betsy), Miss Palmer is very loyal, and once she makes up her mind to something she is unlikely to change it. She enjoys being in the public life, but not to the exclusion of her own privacy. Helping others is a must for unpretentious Betsy Palmer. At times she likes to reminisce and relive childhood experiences. All in all, Betsy has a good outlook on life and she is likely to be wearing a big smile.

12.
Norma Zimmer

Norma Zimmer first saw the light of day in Larson, Idaho. When she was two years old, her family moved to Seattle, Washington. Norma's talent began to surface with her participation in the school glee club and her church choir. This pleased her father and he decided his daughter should direct her energies toward a career. To him this meant delaying marriage as long as possible.

"My father not only didn't want me to get married," she laughs, "he didn't want my mother to teach me to cook or knit or sew. He didn't want me to be domestic at all."

As her popularity progressed, Norma began singing leads in school operettas and performed Sunday after Sunday in the church choir. Then one weekend a girl friend invited Norma along to a mountain cabin at a ski resort. That weekend was to be long remembered, for as Norma and her friend stepped off the bus a certain handsome young man came into her life. The girl friend introduced Randy Zimmer to Norma and it was love at first sight.

Randy was forewarned of Norma's strict father and when the two men met, Randy said just the right words to charm his future father-in-law.

"At that time," recalls Norma, "Randy was a very ambitious fellow who had no intention of marrying, so Dad accepted him right away. I guess Dad didn't consider Randy a threat."

A scholarship at Seattle University had been awarded

Norma, but when the opportunity came for a singing audition in Hollywood she knew she was Hollywood-bound.

"It was a hard decision to make," admits Norma, "but accepting the scholarship would have meant not coming to Hollywood. About the only time I felt free and confident was when I sang.

"Somehow I knew everything was going to be all right. I knew I was going to be a singer. I really prayed over the decision, whether I should go there or stay home and go to school. After much serious thought and prayers, it just seemed I knew I should go to California."

The breaks came and Norma sang with a quartet, "The Girl Friends," which backed almost every top soloist of that time— people like Frank Sinatra, Bobby Darin, and Bing Crosby. Norma also sang the high obbligato on Nat Cole's recording of "Nature Boy."

Next came The Norman Luboff Choir, Voices of Walter Schumann, and other outstanding choral groups.

Later, she married the man of her dreams—Randy Zimmer.

She smiles and says, "I know this sounds crazy, but every year our marriage has become happier. We've had our disappointments, but Randy is pretty wonderful, so our life together has been pretty nearly perfection."

A sincerely devout Christian, Norma confides, "I spend a great deal of my life in prayer. Reading the Bible uplifts me, and I love the books of Dr. Norman Vincent Peale. One of the most treasured gifts I've ever received was a copy of *The Power of Positive Thinking.* Prior to that I'd never read any books of that kind, and it started me on to a better way of thinking.

"I'd just moved to California when a friend sent me the book. She thought it would help me when I was away from my home."

Today Norma Zimmer sings on a telecast from her church, Robert Schuller's Garden Grove Community Church, and on the Lawrence Welk Show, and for Billy Graham Crusades.

"I have never appeared any place without asking God to please help me bring joy to someone. I try to be an instrument of his love.

"People are crying out for a return to the old-time religion, with hymns and the feeling of God. I believe that if we could get back to the old-time religion, then we wouldn't have the problems we do have today."

May God's blessings attend you always,

Blessings,

Norma Zimmer

NORMA ZIMMER

The handwriting of Miss Norma Zimmer, the singer who is known for her appearances on the Lawrence Welk show, where she is known as the "Champagne Lady," points to a person who has a great sense of rhythm and musical ability. Her writing shows balance and control, two qualities which support her when her sensitive and emotional nature would tend to affect her responses. She comes to a decision by gathering all the facts. She is more concerned with taking care of the responsibilities of the present than rushing ahead to the future. She is thrifty, practical, and independent. One who enjoys physical activity, Miss Zimmer usually is on the go, doing her best to get a job well-done.

13.
Your Emotions Are Showing

Do you "blowup" at the slightest provocation, or are you "cool as a cucumber," rarely letting other people know how you feel?

HOW'S YOUR EMOTIONAL RESPONSE? How do you react to a movie with a sad ending? Do you shed tears or do you keep your feelings bottled up inside you, unexpressed? When you hear gossip, are you likely to jump to conclusions, or do you dismiss it from your mind until you are given all the facts of the matter?

FAR FORWARD SLANT WRITING shows a person who is apt to shed tears at a sad movie, and will respond to almost any emotional situation. You respond to people and emotional appeals like flies are attracted to honey. You show others how you feel, and you are ruled by these feelings. You might not express these feelings in words but your "body language" will tell on you. You are sympathetic, affectionate, friendly, and considerate. You carry your heart on your sleeve, and rush headlong into things without thinking of the consequences of your action. But do not think that your emotional expression will hinder your success. Most leaders and people in the theater are highly emotional people who express their feelings outwardly.

//////

People express their feelings in varying degrees. Everyone who cries at a movie will not lose his head in an emergency. Some people are unpredictable in their emotional response.

80

(Top) Joan Hake Robie and Colonel Harland Sanders when they worked together on his book, *Finger Lickin' Good* (Bottom) Darlene Swanson, Betsy Palmer, and Joan at a Billy Graham Crusade

(Top) Pat Boone and Joan break during a meeting. (Bottom) Rex Humbard preaching at The Cathedral of Tomorrow

The late but unforgettable Ethel Waters singing "His Eye Is on the Sparrow"

(Top) Jimmy Carter, President of the United States (Bottom) Jane Withers, star of stage, screen, radio, and television

Evangelist Billy Graham who has influenced millions of people for God

(Top) Joan Winmill Brown, author and actress (Bottom) Cliff Barrows, music director for the Billy Graham team

(Top) Robert H. Schuller, author and minister famed for his "Possibility Thinking" (Bottom) George Beverly Shea, "America's beloved gospel singer"

Singer/actress/author Dale Evans Rogers

(Top) Liz Humbard singing on her father's telecast (Bottom) The Humbard Family Singers in performance

(Top) Norma Zimmer of "The Lawrence Welk Show" (Bottom) Singer Pat Boone

One time they may be very expressive, and another time show no feeling whatsoever. It takes a skilled analyst to decipher this and make the proper evaluation.

VERTICAL WRITING indicates that the writer is objective and poised. He is not impressed by sentimentality, and appeals to him must be made with logic and facts. He is quite unexpressive and will not readily show his inner feelings. He will remain calm, even in the midst of an emergency, and will not show any emotional reaction. He will use judgment when making decisions, and usually, will be ruled by his head rather than his heart. He will not jump into anything before thinking first. He will always ask, "Will it pay?" or "Would this be a wise decision?" ////////

BACKHAND SLANTED WRITING indicates a person who is unresponsive to an emotional appeal. He may feel deeply about something, but in most situations will keep his feelings bottled up. Very few people really get to know him. He might be extremely talented but he will not parade his attributes. He is looked upon as one who is cool, calm, and collected, but he might be concerned about himself and introverted. \\\\\\

SLIGHT SLANT TO THE RIGHT writing indicates a person who is quick to respond with sympathy. He will use good judgment, but is also affected by feelings of the heart. He is of a moderate temperament and mildly expressive. He is friendly, but not too emotionally expressive. //////

EXTREME RIGHT SLANT writing indicates a person who is extremely responsive to emotional experiences. He is never calm or objective, he does not stop to reason, but instead will act impulsively. He will not stop to think things through. He cannot wait for anything. He is sure to form conclusions before he knows the facts of a matter. He will be discouraged one minute and up on a cloud the next. ⁄⁄⁄⁄⁄⁄⁄⁄

VARIABLE SLANT writing that is erratic and consistent gives evidence of inconsistency. The writer varies in his emotional reactions from one moment to another. There is evidence of instability. He is unpredictable, unsettled, spasmodic, and changeable. One time he will be friendly and outgoing and, then, suddenly become withdrawn and remorseful. He is hard to figure out. One cannot predict how he will react in any situation. \\\⁄⁄⁄⁄⁄⁄

OCCASIONAL VARYING OF SLANT writing reveals the writer's desire for variety. He will have spurts of inconsistency. He can grow tired of routine and make a completely diverse move, but, if other traits reveal dependability and consistency, it will be just occasionally that he will have these changes in attitudes and actions. \\\⁄⁄⁄⁄⁄⁄⁄⁄

HOW DEEPLY DO YOU FEEL? Depth is force, force is pressure. The width of blackness of a writing line indicates pressure. It is executed by the writer's own strength, forced on the writing material by the pen. It is assumed that the writer has chosen the type of pen which best suits him. The pressure applied to the writing instrument will determine how much force is applied to that emotional expression. If you have a heavy writing with a far forward slant, you know that the person has a responsiveness of emotions plus lasting feeling.

THE HEAVY WRITER carries scars and the feelings of happiness for a long period of time. He loves beautiful things, refinement, and elegance. He appreciates deep sounds of music, rich color, and pleasant odors. His senses are extremely keen, and he needs richness and luxury to satisfy these strong senses. His capacity for frustration is greater than that of the light-line writer. He is like a blotter, he absorbs emotional experiences. Both sculptors and painters, as well as other artistic people, will show color in their writing. There is a need for expression and it shows in the writing. *Since*

THE LIGHT WRITER will not feel comfortable with a stub-point pen. He won't like the appearance of the writing, since it is different from what he is used to producing. The light-line writer can change his moods and recover from a hurt or offense more quickly than the heavy writer. He doesn't absorb emotional experiences to the same degree as does the heavy writer. He can forgive and forget. He often will engage in small talk, while the heavy-line writer desires meaningful conversation. The one can become involved in relatively shallow and quick-changing interests, while the other prefers adult companionship. *Since*

You might find a person with a vertical writing who will, on occasion, have spells of emotional expression. These outbursts, which will occur only at rare intervals, will come about only as the result of deep emotions which had long been suppressed. This person can be likened to a teakettle placed over a flame with the lid sealed and the spout closed. The steam will cause a leak and the kettle will explode. People who have strong emotions which are kept hidden will, when under stress, act in the same way.

Over a period of time the heavy-line writer may undergo more of a personality change than the light-line writer. Although the heavy writer has long-lasting feelings, the very fact that his emotional experiences are absorbed means that there is a constant changing composite of absorbed feelings.

THE MEDIUM WRITER writes with a medium amount of pressure, and he will retain emotional experiences for a time, but, later they will fade. He is neither one extreme nor the other. *Since*

It has been said that opposites attract, but it takes similarity of personality to produce compatibility. In a recent psychological survey of the factors contributing to marital happiness, it was found that one of the most important factors was similarity of emotional makeup, including strength of the sex drive.

14.
What's Your Beat?

Handwriting is labeled rhythmic if it reveals the repetition and unchanging reappearance of a certain height, pressure, and slant factors, written in a natural, unconscious manner; the rhythm of a specimen is its total display of harmony.

We all have our own individual rhythm which is reflected in our handwriting, thus making it unique. This is one reason the author of a script might be easily recognizable. No handwriting can be mistaken for that of another person when a qualified handwriting analyst is given the opportunity to study it, because it is impossible to counterfeit the rhythm of another person's writing. If there is a strong deviation from the genuine rhythm of a writer, it can be detected that there is a falsification involved.

True artists, profound thinkers, and others of distinction who display individuality of form in their writing usually have rhythm in their writing. A disorder in the flow or rhythm of a writing indicates imbalance, and may indicate some form of illness. Rhythmic writing is steady and harmonious; it will not be restrained or hampered, but will flow freely. Rhythmic writing reveals healthy impulses; unrhythmic writing indicates nervous disturbance, inhibitions, and discord. Evenness, regularity, and rhythm are all indications of the degree to which a writer controls his impulses. Even if there are irregularities, the writing is considered rhythmical if the irregularities occur at regular intervals.

The rhythmic pattern and design of a script can be compared

to design in drawing, sculpture, dancing, and especially music. The emotional effectiveness of music is like the harmony felt in rhythmic handwriting: harmonious music is a joy to hear, rhythmic writing is a delight to behold.

Unrhythmic script doesn't flow; it is stagnant, unsteady, and has uneven spots which catch the eye. Stereotyped or monotonous regularity has no rhythm. Rhythmic writing that has regularity indicates strength of will and perseverence.

When a writing shows letters that are disconnected, the person favors intuition over logic. He often is an impractical or idealistic person. A musician may or may not have it, for in the field of music there are the interpretative artists and the technically accurate musicians. The technically accurate musicians have acquired perfection of execution, but do not put into the music that something which marks them as talented interpreters.

People who write unbroken letters are likely to think literally and logically. They probably scoff at intuition, and reach conclusions slowly and through careful logic. They will not jump to conclusions. Those who connect all of their letters are generally quite practical and precise, but rarely creative or intuitive. Their strength lies in carrying out ideas, not dreaming them up. They might be highly successful in business but it's possible they might fail as an artist, writer, or the like.

When writing has both connected and disconnected letters, the person's thinking is both logical and intuitive. This is how most of us form our letters, and how most of us think. We are logical a large part of the time, but we're guided, too, by intuition. Because most people form connected and unconnected letters, other factors in the writing must be analyzed for clues to their business ability, imagination, and practicality.

People whose writing is never connected are usually quick to perceive ideas and situations. And when disconnected letters appear in very small writing, it's probable that the writer is highly sensitive and introspective as well as imaginative.

When analyzing the writing of someone whose job is routine, but whose script is filled with disconnected letters, look into that person's hobbies. It is likely that he or she expresses creativity and imagination during free time. There are various supportive traits and characteristics which are considered trends toward talent. They are color appreciation, creativity, line value, literary aptitude, cultural interest, musical ability, and artistic ability.

15.
Can You Spot a Criminal?

What kind of person commits a crime?

We have heard the term *criminal type* and most of us have used it more than once in our lifetimes. But did we realize just what we were saying? Quite likely we meant that there are outstanding features or weaknesses of a criminal which make it possible to readily identify him.

There are two types of criminals; those who are antagonistic toward society, and the frustrated type, who are unable to adjust to difficult situations.

It is assumed that the mind regulates behavior. This leads us to ask which mental deviations or mental abnormalities have to do with criminal behavior. A comprehensive knowledge of personality is often one of the keys, or the key to unexplained behavior. A person might not show mental abnormalities, but nevertheless be driven into crime by an unconscious urge.

A criminal commits his own type of crime, depending upon his personality and the circumstances of his existence. A person with a low IQ will, in most cases, commit a lesser offense, such as stealing some insignificant object, that is, unless he is led by someone else. Then anything is possible. A person with a high IQ will commit a crime which is more complicated. It is considered that any criminal act is determined by the personality of the guilty. Statistics have given us ample proof that people who have strength of character, coupled with a deep religious faith, will not be tempted into crime, even under trying circumstances.

We all have social needs and there is no one who is completely devoid of this feeling. The criminal and the neurotic know this and try to justify their deeds in order to shift the responsibility on society and will blame "the establishment." They do not face up to their problem. They have lost courage, and they need to know Jesus Christ as their Savior.

Home environment has much to do with the development of character traits in the young. Weak and overindulgent parents are the producers of weak offspring.

The type of mental disorders most frequently found in criminals are the psychosis, in combination with mental deficiency, schizophrenia, manic-depressive psychosis, and psychopathic inferiority. It seems that mental illness is significant in the cases of crime where feelings of a persecution complex lead the individual to attack his imagined persecutor; where his psychosis makes him feel the need of status, and thereby commits crimes to get attention; and where his psychosis is a substitute for crime in his desire to escape from an intolerable life situation.

An outstanding feature of certain criminals is a frustrated sex drive, and abnormal or warped sex appetites. This is indicated in writing that is blotted and/or has corrugated or rough edges on the strokes. These are always very dangerous signs of a criminal and one should be very wary about such a person.

The insatiable desire for possessions constitutes a very high percentage of crimes among the young and old alike. They lack character enough to fight the temptation to take what doesn't belong to them.

Signs of Dishonesty

Beware of the person whose writing has letters that are open at the base. This is a strong indication of dishonesty and deliberate hypocrisy. An occasional open-base letter can be a slip of the pen, but where the letters are consistently open it is a sign that the writer cannot be trusted.

Other signs of dishonesty are:

(1) Letters that vary in weight and size.
(2) Featheredge letters; uneven pressure.
(3) Snake-like finals (ending stroke).
(4) Curls in first strokes and finals.
(5) Consistently illegible writing.
(6) Exaggerated, artificial writing.
(7) Letters that have been omitted.
(8) Writing that has many corrections.
(9) Small letters with double knots.
(10) First strokes that have been repeated.
(11) More left slant in capitals and finals.

But each of the above is not a conclusive sign of dishonesty. A person's handwriting will often reveal dishonest traits and a skilled analyst will need to make a complete evaluation of the writing before the evidence will conclude that the person is dishonest.

Sometime ago I was privileged to take an intensive course of study in questioned documents. Little did I realize that I would very soon be called upon to use this newfound knowledge. One day my telephone rang and it was the Greenville Police Department. "I read your newspaper column and enjoy it very much," said the police detective. "I wonder if you could help us out on some police matters. It involves a stolen credit card. A professional office building was robbed and a doctor's credit card taken. Then the thief took the doctor's car, which was parked in front of the building. The thief bought gas for the car and paid for it with the stolen credit card. He signed the doctor's name, which was on the credit card. Our suspect denies having done it, but we are pretty sure he's lying. Would you check the signature of the suspect with the one signed for the gas purchase?"

"I'd be glad to help you. Could you get me some "blowups" of the signatures in order to make my work a little easier?"

"Sure. I'll have them made right away," he said.

It took me about sixteen hours of hard work in order to come to a definite conclusion as to the signature identification. Here are some of the things I saw. The J in the name Jerome is very similar to the J in John, which is the suspect's signature. Both J's have very full upper loops, as well as a similarity of length in the lower loops. The beginnings and endings of both J's form a natural arc. Also, there is much similarity in the slant of both signatures. Upon close examination of the remaining letters in both signatures we find that there is sufficient similarity to come to the conclusion that both are the work of one author. And so the report was given to the Greenville Police Department.

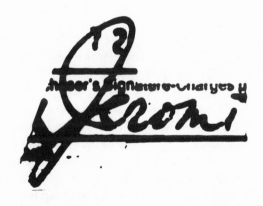

Signature on Gas Purchase Slip

Suspect's True Signature

A few weeks after my work for the Greenville police they called me again and had another identification they wanted made. They produced five checks which were signed with the name Larry Burns. One problem was that Larry Burns was already in jail for another offense and couldn't possibly have written those checks. The person who wrote out the nine checks had access to Larry's apartment and was familiar with his signature. So it was a matter of practice for him to produce a signature that would fool most people. He cashed one of the checks at the supermarket, but when the cashier reviewed the photographs, which are taken automatically with each transaction, she was unable to identify the suspect's photo. So the job of identification was put on my shoulders.

Look at the writing of the real Larry. Then look at the Larry written on the check. Notice how carefully the forger made the letters of the name. They are carefully drawn, and do not flow like the true signature does. This is one thing that a forger cannot do, because the impulses come from our brains and will flow with a certain rhythm which cannot be copied by another person. There are too many "stops" in the questioned signature to have it be the real Larry's signature. Except for people who have certain physical ailments or mental disorders these stops will not appear in a person's writing. Another feature to consider is that the slant of the forger's writing is more vertical than that of the real Larry. This was another thing which the forger did not know to try to conceal.

An analyst is able to save thousands of dollars for people by using his skill for such identification purposes.

Larry's Real Signature

Forged Signature

16.
Colonel Harland Sanders

"I don't believe in retiring!" says Colonel Harland Sanders, of Kentucky Fried Chicken fame, "cause you'll rust out quicker'n you'll wear out."

Colonel Sanders is a "young" eighty-seven-year-old man who has proven that hard work won't hurt anybody. With his white hair and goatee, black string tie, and gem-studded walking stick, he's the perfect caricature of a Southern gentleman.

Sanders is considered to be one of the most successful food franchisers of all time. He is the founder of Kentucky Fried Chicken Corporation, the largest commercial food service chain in the nation, with more than four thousand outlets and sales exceeding seven hundred million dollars annually. Besides taping TV commercials for KFC, he travels over two hundred thousand miles a year as their "goodwill ambassador," appearing in promotional parades and celebrations.

"For years I liked to fool around, cookin' in the kitchen. I had to learn to cook at a very young age. My mother was widowed when I was just five. She had to leave us kids at home in Henryville, Indiana, for weeks at a time while she went to do seamstress work for a family. She'd have to stay there until she had clothes made for all the family.

"One day when I was seven, I decided to bake a loaf of bread. I can remember the wonderful aroma of fresh baked bread when I opened the oven. I thought it was the most beautiful loaf of bread I'd ever seen. At that time mother was working at the Henryville canning factory. I was so proud of that bread that I washed up my kid brother and sister and we walked all the way into town to show the bread to mother. You can be sure we got hugs and kisses from mom and those tomato-pickin' ladies.

"Throughout my lifetime, I was willing to do whatever job I could get—railroad man, streetcar conductor, Army enlistee, justice of the peace, tire salesman, midwife, and ferry boat owner.

"I guess you could say my lucky break came when in 1929 I opened up a filling station in Corbin, Kentucky. The only problem was that my location wasn't as good as a station across the street, owned by a Mr. McVey. I knew I had to do something to get customers, so I got the idea of giving free air. When I had the air compressor put in, I had them dig a trench across the road so McVey could have it too. He appreciated it so much that when he moved, he let me rent his place for $25 a month. My business grew.

"Traveling men were always asking where there was a good place to eat. This gave me the idea of opening up an eating place. My cash on hand was zero, zero, zero. But we had an old family dining room table and six chairs. Our kitchen was equipped with a gasoline stove with four burners, and a 1930 refrigerator with the motor on top. I remember the tank of the stove wouldn't hold pressure, so I had to stand there and pump it while my wife cooked the meal. We'd cook for the five of us and between our meals we'd offer meals to any who came along. I used to sit truck drivers and millionaires down at the same table. It didn't make any difference to me.

"I always served my customers good portions. You can be sure nobody ever went away from my table hungry. If he did, it was his own fault. We'd serve food like fried chicken, country ham, and steaks. Can you believe our steaks only cost $1.75? There always were hot biscuits and honey on the table.

"For years I'd been experimenting with various seasonings until one day I came up with the best tastin' chicken I ever ate, and I began serving it to my customers. They liked it and my business flourished. I built a forty-two-seat restaurant. Later, when it was destroyed by fire, I rebuilt it and added a thirty-five-unit motel.

"I was sittin' on top of the world. I thought I was a good citizen. I was active in church and civic affairs. I did have one vice—it was cussin'. It used to make people mad. I tried to stop it but found that I couldn't.

"Mom taught us to live right—leave off the unclean things like tobacco and alcohol—always go to Sunday School and church. Boy! She was so strict about the Sabbath that when Sunday came around, we weren't even allowed to whistle. Another thing she warned us about was card playin'. She said it would lead to gamblin' and then to trouble. To this day I don't drink or smoke.

"My restaurant had become so popular that it was listed in *Duncan Hines' Adventures in Good Eating.* And Governor Laffoon made me a "Kentucky Colonel," an honor given to outstanding state citizens. The future looked bright.

"Then in 1956, construction was begun on a new interstate highway and it bypassed my cafe by seven miles. It would take a lot of traffic away from the restaurant.

"I realized I had to move quick, so I put my place up for sale. It didn't sell. I finally had to sell it at public auction and I got such a low price for it that by the time I paid off my debts I was almost penniless.

"There I was—sixty-five years old with little more than a Social Security check to live on. I got the idea to try to franchise my recipe for frying chicken. I'd never liked the idea of franchisin' though, because I thought they were all crooks. I'd lost $10,000 one time on a crooked soft ice cream deal. But I knew there was nothing crooked about my deal."

Starting all over again at age sixty-five wasn't easy, but determinedly Sanders loaded the back of his car with a case of

Coca Cola, a container of chicken with crushed ice on top, a fifty-pound lard can filled with seasoned flour, and some pressure cookers. Often sleeping in his car, he visited one restaurant after another, offering to show the owners his method of cooking chicken.

He laughs, "I didn't sell the franchise in those days. I'd give it away. The restaurant owner would buy the cooker from me at my cost. Then we'd agree that he would pay me five cents a head on each chicken sold. He would get my seasoned mixture of spices and herbs. I'd trust him on the honor system, with him keeping the books."

Never revealing the contents of his secret recipe, Colonel Sanders, in seven and a half years, built his business up to what he calls, "a two million proposition."

Then, about seven years ago, Colonel Sanders' life was changed. One day when he was walking down a street in Louisville, two men stopped to speak with him. They invited him to attend a "revival meeting" which was being held in a local church, the Evangel Tabernacle. Much to the surprise of everyone, the Colonel walked into the church that very night.

Reverend Waymon L. Rodgers, pastor of Evangel Tabernacle, greeted Colonel Sanders and invited him into the pastor's study.

"Reverend," asked Colonel Sanders, "do you think a man can get enough religion, or an experience with God, that he could be sure he'd go to heaven when he died?"

The pastor smiled, "Why sure he can."

"You see," continued the Colonel, "I've been looking for an experience with God for more than seventy-five years. But it's never happened to me."

"Colonel," said Rodgers, "let me pray for you. I know you are a blessing to many people, but let me pray that you'll be a spiritual blessing."

"Oh, yes," replied the Colonel tearfully, "please do."

The pastor prayed and they both left the study. Now it was time for the service to begin. As they walked into the sanctuary, there were hundreds of people there. Heads turned to get a glimpse of the celebrity who was walking down the aisle with the pastor.

Turning to the Colonel, Reverend Rodgers said, "Colonel, I want you to sit up on the platform with me."

"Oh, no," gasped the Colonel, in amazement, "I don't want to sit on the platform of a church."

"Well," replied the pastor, "everybody's looking at you anyway. This way, they can see you better."

So up to the platform the two men went, the Colonel clutching tightly the walking stick he held in his left hand, and a huge diamond ring flashing from one finger.

When the visiting evangelist stood to preach, Rodgers and the Colonel left the platform and took seats on the front row of the church. After the sermon, the evangelist asked those who wanted to accept Christ as their Savior to raise their hand.

The Colonel's hand went up.

Noticing this, Pastor Rodgers suggested the two of them get down on their knees and talk with God.

"I don't know what to say," whispered the Colonel, shyly.

"Just repeat what I say, and mean it from your heart," encouraged Rodgers. The prayer went like this—"Dear Lord, I'm a sinner. I need you as my Savior. Please come and live in my heart. I really mean this prayer. In Jesus' name."

As the Colonel prayed, tears dropped down his rugged face. Then, turning to Rodgers, he said, "I have another need, I've been a curser all my life. I've sworn and taken the Lord's name in vain. I've tried to quit this habit but I never could. Do you think God can help me stop the blame cussin'?"

"Sure he can," promised Rodgers. A few minutes elapsed and the Rodgers said, "Colonel, let's pray that God will deliver you from the cursing."

With confidence the Colonel shook his head and said, "No need to do that. He's already heard me."

Before he left the church that night, Colonel Sanders stood to his feet and gave a ten-minute testimony of what God had just done for him.

"I understand now," says the Colonel, "that a man can be a good citizen, join a church, be baptized, and take communion, but unless he's 'born again' he cannot have eternal life.

"I've always wanted to be baptized where Jesus was baptized," Colonel Sanders told Rodgers sometime later. So, in 1971, while on a trip to the Holy Land, the Colonel got his wish. He and Mrs. Sanders, along with some members of Reverend Rodgers' church, were baptized in the Jordan River.

Before Colonel Sanders ever started his franchising business, he prayed, "Dear Lord, if you will make my business a success, I'll see that you have a fair share of it." And he has stayed true to his promise. Throughout the years, 10 percent of his income has gone to religious institutions, and he has given millions to foundations, including some he has set up to help others.

The Colonel has been the recipient of many honors, among them the American Schools and Colleges Association's

Hi Joan, every good wish to you along. Sincerely Col Harland Sanders January 8 - 1972

COLONEL HARLAND SANDERS

Horatio Alger Award in 1965, and an honorary doctor of law degree from Union College, Barbourville, Kentucky, in 1968.

Colonel Sanders chicken is finger-lickin' good and his secret recipe of spices and herbs is locked up in a vault, but there's no secret to his experience with Christ. He'll tell you that!

Age makes no difference to Colonel Sanders. At age eighty-plus, his physical drive, persistence, and determination could outweigh most young men. Colonel Sanders likes responsibility and work and he has no patience with a "lazy loafer." With his imagination, he moves ahead to accomplish the almost impossible. He will analyze and investigate a problem until he has solved it. He believes in total commitment and is loyal to what he believes is right. A true actor, his vanity is nourished by the love and attention he receives—especially from "the little ones." Although he strives to be objective his heart usually rules his head.

CLAUDIA SANDERS

A gentle, sensitive, and loving wife, Claudia Sanders, wife of Colonel Harland Sanders, is usually content to remain in the background and let her husband get the attention from the crowds. In spite of this, however, she reaches out for warmth, love, and security. But do not be misled. Behind that shy and quiet disposition is a strong and purposeful woman. When people gather around her husband and stay too long, she is likely to whisper to her husband in no uncertain tone, "Let's go, H. D."

17.
Kathryn Kuhlman

The lights dim, the spotlight sweeps the stage dramatically, as faith healer, Evangelist Kathryn Kuhlman, radiating energy, moves her slender body back and forth across the stage.

Creating an attitude of worship, with the help of two pianos and an organ, Miss Kuhlman leads the audience in singing the chorus, Hallelujah. Hext she tells them news about the miracles which are occurring every day as Jesus' coming gets nearer. She calls up to the stage several guests present who have been healed at previous services.

When the healings begin, she says, "Thank you, Jesus. Oh! That's great, Jesus!" When people get all excited over what is happening and rush to thank her, she announces dramatically, "Don't thank me, honey. Thank Jesus."

Kathryn Kuhlman was born in Concordia, Missouri, a little town about sixty miles from Kansas City. Her father was the town's mayor. Concordia boasted of three small churches—Methodist, Baptist, and Lutheran. Miss Kuhlman was raised in the Methodist church, but later converted to her father's Baptist beliefs.

"We weren't tremendously religious," says Miss Kuhlman, "but in a small town the church always plays an important part in people's lives. One Sunday when I was fourteen years old, I was in church with Mama. During the last song of the service, as I was holding the hymnal, I began to shake. I laid the hymnal down and I began to weep. They weren't tears of sorrow, but I didn't know why I was crying. I didn't know what to do, but something drew me to the front pew. I sat down. A crippled lady gave me her handkerchief and told me not to cry.

"It was only later that I found that it was the Holy Spirit that was with me that day. But following my spiritual experience, all I knew was that I wanted to serve.

"I believed that I had been born without talent. So when I had my spiritual experience I finally knew that I was going to have some use. Because I had little talent of my own I could consecrate myself totally to God. I could give myself to him completely, and be his instrument."

At sixteen years of age, Kathryn Kuhlman said she was called by the Lord to the ministry. She taught herself the Bible, then began preaching, and developed a nondenominational following. Calling herself "the handmaiden of the Lord," she said she was not a minister or a religious leader.

In 1948 she came to the town of Franklin in western Pennsylvania where she conducted weekly religious services. After followers claimed to be healed of illnesses at the touch of her hand she was barred from using the Gospel Tabernacle there.

From that location the evangelist moved to Oil City where she built a 2,000 seat temple. Later, she presented the temple as a gift to the residents in the area and moved to First Presbyterian Church in Pittsburgh where she maintained her headquarters until her death.

Since 1967, Kathryn Kuhlman confined her work to a weekly service in Pittsburgh, with a monthly sermon at the Shrine Auditorium in Los Angeles, where she regularly drew crowds of seven thousand or more. On an average she held one hundred and twenty-five healing services per year and reached approximately one and a half million people needing healing. It was a usual sight to see hordes of people lining up in front of auditoriums before the light of dawn to be assured of getting inside the buildings where Kathryn Kuhlman would be preaching. Miss Kuhlman has written three books and has been the subject of numerous magazine articles and books.

"I always worry that sometime I may go out on the stage and find that the Holy Spirit has decided not to use me as his instrument any longer. But I do know why miraculous healings are occurring. God does the healing. I only show the people faith. In the Bible Christ says, 'If you won't believe me, believe my miracles.'

"Miracles, healings, are Christ's way of telling us to prepare for him. There are more miraculous healings now, in the 1970s, than there have been at any other time since the days of the early church." Hallelujah!

On February 20, 1976, after heart surgery complications, seventy-three-year-old Miss Kathryn Kuhlman went to be with her Lord.

Please accept my appreciation and may God give you a Christmas that is blessed with all the good things that He has reserved for His children...

KATHRYN KUHLMAN

Although she was a woman of vision and mystery, Kathryn Kuhlman's life and actions were under firm control. (Notice the invisible base line which the writing follows.) But, in spite of the stability and self-assurance, there was a great need to be wanted and loved. She was extremely intelligent and possessed exceptionally good powers of concentration and creativity. Her place of ministry required appearing before thousands of people, but she relished the times when she could get alone and away from the crowds. Kathryn Kuhlman was loyal to what she believed. She was independent, determined, and forthright. She had a strong will, but also a nature which often would yield to the wishes of others. Her sense of rhythm expressed itself in the long flowing dresses she wore and the way she would glide across a floor. (Notice the even flow of the writing.) This is a sample of an unusual writing and an unusual person.

18.
Their Writing Talks

Cliff Barrows
Dave Boyer
Bill Brown
Joan Winmill Brown
President Jimmy Carter
Judson Cornwall
Andraé Crouch
Richard M. DeVos
David DuPlessis
Joni Eareckson
Billy Graham
Ruth Graham
Hansi
Al Hartley
The Hawaiians
Charles Hunter
Frances Hunter
Elisabeth Elliot Leitch
Pat Robertson
George Beverly Shea
Jimmy Swaggart
Ethel Waters
David Wilkerson

CLIFF BARROWS

A huge choir before him makes Cliff feel the sense of achievement he enjoys. He has lots of physical stamina and self-confidence (long lower loop on y and underlining of name). He likes to maintain his privacy and when he does reach out to others it is with caution. Then he is likely to pull back a little. (Look at the final or ending of the name, Barrows. Notice how it seems to fade away and then pull to the left. The pull to the left is an inward pull.) He is somewhat protective of those he loves (C in Cliff which envelopes the rest of the letters. B in Barrows envelopes the rest of the letters of the last name).

DAVE BOYER

The sky is the limit for gospel musician Dave Boyer's aspirations (high up-strokes on the capital S in Sincerely as well as the up-strokes on the last line of the writing). The round and full capitals on the indistinguishable D which looks like an O and the B on Boyer show his love for responsibility. Dave enjoys analyzing and investigating a situation (wedges in n in Sincerely and first word of the last line). Rhythm is expressed in the flow of the entire body of the writing. The figure 8 in his signature (second line) indicates cultural interest. He selects a few intimate friends. To most people he keeps an air of mystery about himself. One who likes to take the shortcut route, Dave doesn't like to be worried with too many details. This highly emotional man is apt to let his heart rule his head in an emotional situation.

The Lord is good !

William F. Brown

BILL BROWN

Full of enthusiasm, high ideals, and a love for life, Bill Brown likes to be on the go (expansive and high letters). He must have lots of room to move. He is sensitive and has a concern for the feelings of others. But he resists any impositions anyone might place on him. Upstroke, (first stroke of B in Brown) is firm and straight which indicates the resistance. Bill likes to investigate and explore. He is somewhat impatient. (Jabs and points in various places of the writing.) He is a logical thinker who is moved by his emotional experiences. He is a kind and gentle man. All in all a good balance of qualities.

I trust in the power of Jesus Christ.

Joan M. Brown.

JOAN WINMILL BROWN

Joan Winmill Brown is an author and actress. She has great creative talent. Although a very intense individual, Joan is extremely levelheaded. Her thinking is logical and literal (straight, vertical letters). But in spite of the logical and literal thinking, she is keenly intuitive and sensitive to her surroundings. She is an independent thinker who can at times be somewhat inflexible. Joan is apt to hold most people at arm's length (wide spaces between words). Culture and the finer, creative arts are of tremendous interest to her.

PRESIDENT JIMMY CARTER

Stability and a nonvacillating nature help make President Jimmy Carter one who is not likely to do anything rash. (The y in Jimmy and the way the t is crossed in Carter let us know how analytical is his mind. Any move he makes is done after the situation is carefully studied.) He is cautious, determined, and sensitive. (Sensitivity is indicated by the open loop in the t.) Mr. Carter's heavy pressure on the pen reveals his deep feelings. The absence of a loop on the y tells us that he needs and wants privacy. Because he is a very conservative person, Jimmy Carter is not likely to make emotional decisions. The high "t-bar" above the capital J in Jimmy stands for vision and spirituality. What we have seen thus far in the public life of Jimmy Carter would undoubtedly fortify the belief that the above analysis is true of the man and president, Jimmy Carter.

JUDSON CORNWALL

Bible teacher Judson Cornwall likes the ornate and elaborate, and attention to himself (frills in the writing). The intertwining of the writing and the bottom letters of the writing, which run into the top of the letters on the lower lines, tell us that he maintains some mystery about himself. The elaborate writing also is an attempt to cover up some feelings of insecurity (tiny lowercase letters in Judson and Cornwall). Mr. Cornwall appreciates cultural and intellectual things (Greek-looking capital E and figure 8 in the capital T in To). There is a desire to protect, if not overpower others (huge double-lined C in Cornwall over small lowercase letters. Also the E in Eph.). Mr. Cornwall has physical drive which needs some expression.

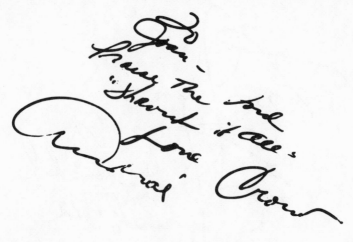

ANDRAÉ CROUCH

Musical genius Andraé Crouch must have plenty of room in which to move. Confinement could be his worst enemy. He is a lover of variety and change; it is difficult to predict his next move. Since he cannot be bogged down with too many details, he is likely to gather surface information and let the details be worked out by someone else. This is fine for Andraé, since he doesn't always finish what he begins. His "Big Daddy" nature is the reason for his desire to protect others and to take charge. (This is shown in the large, covering A in Andraé.) He is like the umbrella company—he offers protection and security to his friends and family. But he needs to guard against being taken advantage of for his generosity. The broad-topped letter r's give evidence of his generous nature and manual dexterity (strength in his hands). He is apt to speak his mind with great conviction. The pressure and slant of his writing are other indications of his emotional and expressive nature. Andraé Crouch enjoys rich color and rich food. A likeable guy!

RICHARD M. DEVOS

Amway Corporation's guru of free enterprise, Mr. Richard M. DeVos, is a business leader who maintains firm but heartfelt control over his constituents. His individuality, vision, creativity, and showmanship attribute to his financial success. There is a desire for responsibility, indicated by the large open R in Richard. Showmanship is expressed in the flowing free capital letters. The variety of slant in the name indicates that DeVos is versatile, not rigid; able to change his plans or direction, perhaps to line up with others' wishes. He is warm and friendly but in a reserved sort of way. A sensitive individual who does not always want to be in the limelight, Mr. DeVos has a combination of qualities which make him someone you'd like to know.

To Joan
Rom 8:26-28
David J. du Plessis

DAVID DUPLESSIS

A lover of responsibility (large, full capital letters), DuPlessis is enthusiastic and optimistic (long and ascending T-bar). His self-confidence is evident from the underlining of his name. He is more interested in spiritual than temporal things. He reveals independent thinking by his short-topped, lowercase *d* in David. Mr. DuPlessis has a variety of interests. There is also a certain gentility about him. (Perhaps it is due, in part, to his geographical location of birth and upbringing.) He is friendly to others, but has some reservations about responding to someone he doesn't know.

JONI EARECKSON

Joni Eareckson's physical limitations are by no means any indication of mental or emotional limitations. This bright, energetic young woman, paralyzed from the neck down as a result of a diving accident, exhibits in her writing (mouth writing) an alert mind which is always eager to learn. (Greek E's letter formations and the flow of her writing indicate a desire for learning.) The enthusiasm, as revealed in the crossing of the T in To, coupled with the "confidence" line drawn under "To Joan," are only a small part of the make-up of this creative young woman. Her self-assurance and determination undoubtedly account for her success as a speaker and head of her own company which sells the prints and stationery bearing her artwork. Her vertical writing and the heavy pressure with which she applies the pen to the paper announce her deep emotions which are controlled by literal and logical thinking. Emotional experiences are rarely forgotten by Joni, who keeps her own confidence. She is a bundle of creativity which cannot be confined. It must grow and expand.

BILLY GRAHAM

This twentieth-century religious leader is both spiritual and mysterious. The effects of emotional experiences are long-lasting. His vision is far-reaching and, coupled with his determination, he usually reaches his goals. His emotional depth and dynamic self-expression give his followers a satisfying sense of security. His likes responsibility and this is evidenced by the take-charge, in-control way he delivers his sermons. (Notice the large B.) Dr. Graham has no difficulty taking any situation in hand, especially when it involves the protection of his and others' interests. This unusual man requires a large area in which to move and to express himself. His spacious, secluded home in the South gives him privacy and the space he so desperately desires. Cetainly, he is not one who likes long periods of confinement. When he is confined, he is planning his move back to another gigantic crusade. (This specimen of Dr. Graham's writing was obtained just as he was heading out to preach at one of his crusades. He, of course, was under some tension at the time. This specimen, therefore, is not his usual signature. Nevertheless, it does reveal much about his personality.)

MRS. RUTH GRAHAM

Mrs. Ruth Graham, wife of Dr. Billy Graham, is a most intuitive person with a keen sense of rhythm. Her writing indicates an unusual imagination, artistic talent, and appreciation of literature. A lover of responsibility, she will take pride in her work and enjoy showmanship, but never to the point of being pushy. Although the body of the handwriting slants backward, Mrs. Graham is not one to retreat but will speak out with firmness if the situation calls for it. Moves are made with caution. Except for the few times when she can be extravagant, she will always be in complete control of her actions.

To Joan with love!

Psalm 37

Hansi - Maria

HANSI

Authoress Hansi-Maria needs to be loved and wanted and thrives on the attention she gets. (Notice the "heart" under the exclamation point after the word *love;* and the upswing on the upper part [zone] of the letter J in Joan. These are both appeals for attention). But Hansi strives to be objective and keep a level head, maintaining a safe distance from others (space between words). She can be frank and outspoken and persist in reaching her desires (tied loop on the H in capital H means persistence; open a in Joan means frankness). Although she is concerned with the present (large, rounded, "middle-zone" letters), Hansi is very intuitive (breaks between letters) and spiritual.

ing you in such an exciting way.

Warmest regards in Christ,

Al Hartley

ALAN HARTLEY

Alan Hartley, creator of many "Archie" comics, is one who has the ability to "dream" up amusing creations and make them appealing to young and old alike. He is one who expresses his feelings which are deep and real. He is not a person who likes a humdrum existence but enjoys variety and excitement. He will stick to a job once he begins, and his determination is long-lasting.

THE HAWAIIANS

Mark and Diane Yasuhara, known as "The Hawaiians," have plenty of enjoyment from their singing careers. Of the two, Diane is the yielding person (open bottom of the letter s in Jesus). She gathers information which interests her and skims over the rest (dish-shaped bar in the strokes connecting the two names; all the writing is that of Diane except the name "Mark" which appears at the bottom of the page). She is full of life and enthusiasm and likes to have plenty of room to express herself. The signature of Mark (at bottom) indicates that he is apt to be impatient, always in a hurry—on-the-go. His ambitions are high and far-reaching and he is sure of himself (underlining of name). He is one who explores and investigates something before he makes a move. If he ever makes a move without taking time to think, it is only because of his emotional nature.

8/17/3

God is really Fabulous

Praise Jesus

Charles ♡ Frances
Hunter

CHARLES HUNTER

Like his wife, Frances, Charles Hunter is enthusiastic, warm, and friendly. He too, reaches out to others for love and affection. (Notice the long and reaching-up finals or ending strokes on the words, Fabulous, Jesus, Charles, and Hunter.) The heart drawing which always accompanies the signatures of Charles and Frances is another bid for attention. Charles is more likely to express his true feeling and emotions than is his wife. He is possessive of those he loves. (See the circle which begins the name, "Charles.") One who likes responsibility, Charles can at times take on more work than he should. He likes to have control and move ahead with an eye for greater achievement. He can be a little extravagant, but Frances is likely to temper this tendency in him.

FRANCES HUNTER

Exhuberant, enthusiastic Frances Hunter is warm and friendly to those she meets. She reaches out to others for love and affection. (Notice the long and reaching-up final or ending stroke on the word "Frances.") Frances gets a lot of attention in the work she does, and she enjoys every minute of it. Nevertheless, she is somewhat of a private person who will gain strength in the times when she is able to be alone. Her thinking is logical and objective, and she has good powers of concentration. (The letters of Frances, the "r,a,n,c,e,s," are all small in size. They are concentrated, connected letters which indicate logical and objective thinking.) Frances is not likely to skip over any details. Her choice of clothes and furnishings for her home is not likely to be too lavish but simple and in good taste. Frances has much respect for the traditional.

Hi Joan !

*"When thou passest through the waters, I will be with thee ...
(Look it up in Isaiah 43)*

Elisabeth Elliot Leitch

ELISABETH ELLIOT LEITCH

Elisabeth Elliot Leitch is full of enthusiasm and vision. (Look at the long T-bars crossed above the T-stem.) She is very creative and appreciates learning and cultural endeavors (artistic writing and Greek E's). She has good powers of concentration (small, well-formed letters). The "hurried" appearance of the writing indicates that Mrs. Leitch's mind works quicker than her pen. (Some T-bars appear to rush ahead of the rest of the writing.) The light, delicate writing is an indication of her spirituality and gentility. She is known for her best-selling books like *Under the Shadow of the Almighty*.

Sincerely yours,

Pat Robertson
President

PAT ROBERTSON

An extremely intense man whose emotions run deep, Pat Robertson is one who gets down to the business at hand. This same intensity is carried throughout every phase of his life. He enjoys rich color, food, the finer things of life (heavy pressure of the writing). Highly selective, he will pursue only those endeavors which really interest him or he feels are important. If he is not interested in something, he is apt to skim over the surface and move on to something which he enjoys more. He is full of initiative, enthusiasm, persistence, and determination. He is staunchly loyal to what he believes (the retraced t and d stems). He believes his abilities and limits are boundless. Because he can be unpredictable (variable slant in the writing), others around him are usually unaware of his next move. Sometimes he speaks out in "no uncertain words" (rather pointed right end of t-bar's). Although his work involves people, he does not allow anyone to invade his private world. He retains a few close friends. His creativity lies in the abstract and he strives to reach into the heavenly (tall t-stems and upper-zone letters).

GEORGE BEVERLY SHEA

This warm and friendly man possesses an intense and deeply emotional nature (heavy pressure of the writing). He has high aspirations and appreciates his audience. He is one who will meet another on fair ground and will, when he thinks it necessary, yield to another's opinion or desire. He also can be mysterious and keep people guessing (intertwining of letters). His colorful and expensive tastes are evident in the colorful and flamboyant writing. Mr. Shea feels secure and confident in himself (underlining of the name). A real showman!

JIMMY SWAGGART

Jimmy Swaggart, TV's singing evangelist, is hard to pin down. He is always busy. In a hurry. On the go. (Notice the flurry of the writing which moves toward the right.) His great enthusiasm is evident in the long, sweeping T-bars and the top of the J in Joan.) His visionary and spiritual qualities are shown in the T-bar which is high above the stem and the upper line or bar which is above the J-stem. Although his work and ministry take him among the crowds and in the limelight, Jimmy Swaggart is a private person who desires to keep his personal life from the public eye. (Indicated by the intertwining and closing-in of the signature.) He is not afraid to speak his mind. It is difficult to predict the mood or action of this personality.

ETHEL WATERS

The late Ethel Waters gained fame as a "blues" singer years ago with her rendition of "Stormy Weather." For the last years of her life she sang for the Billy Graham crusades. She revealed great emotional depth in her writing (heavy, and slanted to the right). Because of these deep feelings, Miss Waters retained the effects of an emotional experience for a long time. She did not always outwardly express these feelings. She would seek out information about those subjects which interested her. She was concerned with the things at hand. This "down-to-earth" lady liked simplicity, and basically was a practical person. She had an active imagination. (Notice broad, rather heavy letters.) Being sensitive, she was sure to protect those persons or possessions which she held dear. Miss Waters liked plenty of room in which to move (words spread out over page). At times she would be a little extravagant but in later years, she became more practical and used good judgment. A true showperson, Ethel Waters enjoyed her audience. Her joy and excitement were contagious, but even so, she liked to maintain a certain poise and withdrawal from the public eye. In recent years she was known for her rendition of "His Eye Is on the Sparrow."

For God so loved the world — he gave his only Son — that whosoever believeth on Him should not perish —

David Wilkerson

DAVID WILKERSON

A very serious-minded man, David Wilkerson looks at life with an objective, though sensitive, eye. His every move is with much thought and extreme caution. His is apt to be straightforward—not fearing to speak his mind, even though he might have to stand alone. He enjoys the simple things of life—home and family more than the glory of being before a large crowd. He possesses versatility and you cannot always predict his next move. When possible, he likes to take shortcuts rather than be bogged down with details. (The variability in the writing reveals his versatility.) You cannot always know what kind of emotional response you will get from him. Although he is of a firm mind, he is also able to, when he thinks it is necessary, yield to the wishes of others—but *only* when he feels it is necessary.

19.
True Confessions

The board of deacons of our church is made up of quite a variety of people. Some have rather "hot" tempers which they constantly must keep "under," others tend to be too agreeable, not challenging anyone or anything, and still others can be part of both kinds. Our last board meeting was one which will long be remembered. Tempers got out of control. Feelings were hurt. The pastor had to admonish the deacons to act as Christians should act. This was when I got an idea.

Our deacons and their wives were planning a winter ski retreat at Lake Placid. I knew that they needed better insight into each other's personalities so I suggested that I teach them the eight basic steps of graphoanalysis. Most of them were very eager to learn a little about the science of handwriting analysis so plans were made.

"I can't see how handwriting analysis can be of any use to me!" growled Mrs. Conway, a deacon's wife who had been the cause of some of the friction in the church.

"Come on, Marilyn," admonished her husband, Charles. "You'll enjoy it if you'll only give it a try." He coughed nervously and continued, "Maybe it will help you in your relationships within the church."

Marilyn Conway did have lots of difficulties in her interpersonal relationships. She was a committed Christian but still battled with her personality. I felt very happy and contented thinking about the basic steps course I would be teaching. I realized how important deacons are to a church. There are times when they are faced with decisions and personality conflicts. Being made aware of each other's personality traits, as well as their own, would give them some valuable tools to use in the performance of their church duties. They would learn much about how to work together. Learning and praying were sure to win the battle for the deacons.

The trip to the mountains was enjoyable. We traveled in several carloads. Marilyn was her usual self—didn't like the restaurant we stopped at, the trip was too long, she was tired. On and on she went.

I was really eager to get a sample of Marilyn's handwriting. It would be very enlightening to get to know how her personality operated. I would understand something of her fears and perplexities. Once out in the open and admitted, these fears and perplexities could be dealt with.

Snow began to fall as we headed northward. The four-hour ride would soon be over. We looked forward to a great weekend, but now we were more interested in getting settled at the lodge. Tomorrow would be time enough to begin our skiing. Tonight we would relax by the warm fire and I would give my deacons and their wives a little preview of what we would be studying in our basic steps course. But we all were tired from our day of preparation and the trip. Soon we grew sleepy and, after a time of devotions, we all said good-night.

The next morning we were treated to a scrumptious breakfast of pancakes, sausage, orange juice, and coffee. After we had eaten to our heart's content, we went into a seminar room to begin our studies.

The first session was spent in getting familiar with the instrument used to measure slant of a writing and to talk about the various categories we would be studying; things like goals, aptitudes, the processes of the mind, and the defenses we use. Mrs. Conway was her usual self; impatient and short-tempered, always wanting to rush ahead of the class.

When we looked into the emotional responses of a person, how deeply he feels about experiences, and how he expresses them, Mrs. Conway took a good look at herself. She got more insight into her sensitivity and decided to make a real effort to help herself. She decided it was time to let the Lord take that temper and give her a sweetness and godliness she'd never had before. She saw how silly she'd acted when things didn't go her way.

Deacon Brown, a jolly, good-natured man who always has a smile for everyone, realized that he was just a pushover in his easygoing, give-in way. He needed to firm up and take a stand when he believed in something. He would no longer let a dominant personality overpower any worthwhile ideas or opinions he might have.

Staunch, conservative Mrs. Johnson never could understand why things in the church couldn't be done the way they'd been done for the past fifty years. She hadn't liked the idea of the church sponsoring a "coffee house" for its young people. "We never had a coffee house when I was growing up," she argued. One thing for sure, Mrs. Johnson obviously doesn't like change, and it was no easy task to convince her that she had a problem along this line. She needed to be convinced that she must be more flexible and take change in her stride. She did promise, however, that she would make an effort, with God's help, to improve this part of her personality. Her husband was very supportive and did his best to help her achieve her goal.

A few days later, the end of the ski weekend, I gave each student a handwriting to analyze. Unbeknown to them, the handwritings were that of another person of the group. "This will be the acid test," I thought. "If they are able to analyze each other's handwritings, they will believe that graphoanalysis is a true science and that what they see in each other's writing is really how they are."

A roar of laughter swept across the room as each person read the analysis he'd done. They immediately recognized who it was and were amazed that another person could figure them out. The handwritings did not lie.

By the final day of our study each student viewed the others in a different light. In the months that followed I watched as they put to the test the knowledge they had attained. This, coupled with God's help, brought about revolutionary changes in attitudes and actions. The deacons' meetings took on an air of love and understanding. Isn't that what it's all about?

Joan H. Robie, skilled author/grapho-analyst, gives tips on graphoanalysis. She also presents her analyses of many outstanding celebrities' handwriting, including President Jimmy Carter, Dale Evans Rogers, Pat Boone, Colonel Harland Sanders, Robert Schuller, Betsy Palmer, and others.

Author Robie distinguishes between *graphoanalysis* (her skill) and graphology. *Graphoanalysis,* she says, is a science. The basis of the accuracy of graphoanalysis is that of strokes. The revealing factor into the personality of the writer lies in the strokes of his writing and not the letter formations. She also says it doesn't matter what language the writing is in—even shorthand tells about the writer.

Learn how to analyze your handwriting and that of others. This book also deals with the writing of those with personality disorders and aberrations.